MILLENNIAL KOSHER

recipes reinvented for the modern palate

Recipes and photos by
Chanie Apfelbaum
creator of BUSY IN BROOKLYN

Published by **ARTSCROLL / SHAAR PRESS**
4401 Second Avenue / Brooklyn, NY 11232 / (718) 921-9000 / www.artscroll.com

Distributed in Israel by **SIFRIATI / A. GITLER**
POB 2351 / Bnei Brak 51122 / Israel

Distributed in Europe by **LEHMANNS**
Unit E, Viking Business Park, Rolling Mill Road Jarrow, Tyne and Wear / NE32 3DP, England

Distributed in Australia and New Zealand by **GOLDS WORLD OF JUDAICA**
3-13 William Street / Balaclava, Melbourne 3183, Victoria / Australia

Distributed in South Africa by **KOLLEL BOOKSHOP**
Northfield Centre, 17 Northfield Avenue Glenhazel 2192 / Johannesburg, South Africa

ISBN-10: 1-4226-2055-7 / ISBN-13: 978-1-4226-2055-7

Printed in Canada

To my husband, Yossi, and our children
Nechama, Esther, Ari, Peretz, and Rosie,
for always believing in me.

And in loving memory of my big brother,
Ari Halberstam HY"D,
for teaching me to believe in myself.

לע״ן התמים הקדוש
אהרן יוסף הי״ד בן חנניה סיני דוד שיחי׳ הלברשטם

Table of
CONTENTS

ACKNOWLEDGMENTS

- With thanks to **Hashem** for giving me the strength to overcome so many obstacles and instilling in me the indefatigable drive to make my dreams come true.

- To my husband, **Yossi**, for seeing the good in everything and for helping me see it too.

- To my beautiful children, **Nechama**, **Esther**, **Ari**, **Peretz**, and **Rosie**. For being my taste testers, my cheerleaders, and my pride and joy. You are my everything.

- To my dear **Bubby Hecht**, who passed away just a few months before my book went to print. Thank you for believing in me, even when I put cheese and (pareve) gravy on potato latkes, and for all of your love and support throughout my journey.

- To **Ma**, for showing me by example what it means to never give up on your dreams. You are my greatest role model.

- To my mother-in-law, **Mrs. Sara Apfelbaum**, for opening my eyes to a new food culture, and for serving it up with love.

- To my sister **Sara**, for being my sounding board, my proofreader, and my most fervent supporter.

- To **Leah Schapira**, **Melinda Strauss**, **Naomi Nachman**, **Paula Shoyer**, and **Miriam Pascal**; this book would not be here if not for your continued feedback, guidance, and knowledge. Thank you for sharing and caring every step of the way.

- To **Chaya Suri Leitner**, **Shushy Turin**, **Danielle Renov**, **Sina Mizrachi**, and all my blogger friends who have supported me throughout this process and beyond.

- To **Chana Blumes**, thank you for all your input and your help with photo editing. Your talent is unparalleled!

- To **Dina Gorodetsky**, your friendship means so much to me. Thank you for being a part of this journey.

- To the **Bryskis** and all the **taste-testers of Inner Circle** for all the feedback on my recipes.

- To **Rabbi Gedaliah Zlotowitz**, for believing in my vision and for your willingness to try something new. Thank you for making me feel like family.

- To **Felice Eisner**, for your keen attention to detail and your expertise in refining and perfecting the written word. Thank you for teaching the blogger in me how to write a recipe properly.

- To **Tova Ovits** and **Judi Dick** for your assistance with proofreading.

- To **Devorah Cohen**, for your ability to capture my perspective and put it on the page. Your talent shines through this book.

- To the talented **Abbey Wolin**, for the endleaf design.

- To **Marnie Levy**, for being the perfect hand model, and for all your help in and out of the kitchen.

- To **Chanie Nayman** and the team at *Mishpacha* magazine; I'm so grateful to be a part of such a talented group of women.

- To **Miriam Rosenthal**, for organizing the recipe testing, and to all my amazing **recipe testers**, who helped ensure that each recipe was perfect:

Judith Abittan Banon ▪ Chaya Abrahams ▪ Ashlene Azulay ▪ Dorya Barth ▪ Briana Bayar ▪ Shana Beren ▪ Estee Berkowitz ▪ Rebecca Bernstein ▪ Hannah Berry ▪ Reva Blander ▪ Rivkie Blau ▪ Bayla Blumstein ▪ Cyndi Bodner ▪ Ruthy Bodner ▪ Cami Bouskila ▪ Esther Braun ▪ Shoshana Brenenson ▪ Zeesie Breuer ▪ Frayda Brown ▪ Leah Chaiton ▪ Randy Cohen ▪ Avital Davidi ▪ Khaya Eisenberg ▪ Chaya Elbaum ▪ Naomi Elberg ▪ Ady Fox ▪ Aliza Getz ▪ Chaya Surie Goldberger ▪ Dina Gorodetsky ▪ Sara Gorodetsky ▪ Mindy Gotesman ▪ Ahuva Gottdiener ▪ Sara Gutnick ▪ Chanie Hagege ▪ Ruchie Hersko ▪ Jenny Hollander ▪ Rachel Jacobs ▪ Rachel Jaradeh ▪ Esther Kadosh ▪ Shira Kalish ▪ Inbal Khabieh ▪ Ariella Kirshblum ▪ Esti Kleinbart ▪ Esti Lamm ▪ Shifra Landowne ▪ Mashi Laufer ▪ Miri Lazarescu ▪ Chaya Suri Leitner ▪ Mia Lelonek ▪ Estee Levine ▪ Erica Levy ▪ Marnie Levy ▪ Sheina Liberow-Kavka ▪ Chana Leah Margolis ▪ Esti Mochkin ▪ Naomi Nachman ▪ Shaindy Niederman ▪ Tobie Nussbaum ▪ Zahava Pfeffer ▪ Chaya Piatt ▪ Chana Esther Plotnik ▪ Dorre Reiss ▪ Hailey Remer ▪ Danielle Renov ▪ Miri Rosen ▪ Daniella Rosenberg ▪ DY Rubin ▪ Esther Chana Schechter ▪ Melissa Schon ▪ Kayla Schwarcz ▪ Ahuva Schwartz ▪ Sori Schwartz ▪ Rachel Shapiro ▪ Amy Sheib ▪ Paula Shoyer ▪ Shaindy Siff ▪ Shira Silverman ▪ Yehudis Simons ▪ Devora Singer ▪ Rachel Snado ▪ Liora Stark ▪ Kira Sunshine ▪ Chana Susskind ▪ Yitzi Taber ▪ Bassie Tauby ▪ Shushy Turin ▪ Libby Weiss ▪ Molly Yeh ▪ Michal Zisquit ▪ Raizel Zucker

- Last but certainly not least, the biggest thank-you goes out to all **my fans** and **followers** from around the world who feed my foodie fire and inspire me to be bigger and better! Your personal messages, photos, and constant encouragement mean the world to me.

INTRODUCTION

Growing up, I never wanted anything to do with the kitchen. My older sister would help out with dinner, and I'd happily iron the tablecloth or fold the laundry, just as long as I could stay out of the kitchen. When I was a teenager, it was my job to prep the salads for Shabbos lunch, and I always seemed to mess up the salad dressing. One week, I accidentally used salt instead of sugar in the recipe; it's a wonder that I ever became a food blogger!

I came to food by means of presentation. When I was first married, I didn't have much of a choice but to put supper on the table, so I did it. My food wasn't especially good or especially bad, but when it came to hosting Shabbos guests, presentation was where I shone. I'm not an artist by any means, but I always enjoyed playing around with colors and layout. I like crafting — scrapbooking and crocheting in particular — so it's no surprise that I came to food by way of styling. Of course, food styling was an entirely different ball game when I was first married. Food blogs were in their infancy, and sites like Foodgawker and Tastespotting didn't exist. There were no marble slabs or wooden boards, and we actually enjoyed our food without posting it on social media!

I began to look forward to my weekly Shabbos feasts, and I planned my menu days in advance. Instead of thinking about the food in terms of flavor, I thought about the colors on the table and how they complemented each other. When my guests starting asking for my recipes, I realized that I had ignited a passion I never knew existed and I was excited to explore it. I started to follow food blogs, collect cookbooks, and read food magazines in my spare time.

Fast forward a few years, and three kids later, I was ready to quit my job as a web designer. I wanted to be a stay-at-home mom, but I also needed an outlet for my creative energy. My husband suggested that I start a blog (he came up with the name!), and in 2011, Busy in Brooklyn, or BIB for short, was born. My tagline back then was "cooking, crafting, and coping" and I shared tidbits of my life as a mom of three, my passion for crocheting, and of course, my love of cooking traditional Jewish foods. Like many hobbies that had come and gone through the years, I thought Busy in Brooklyn would be a passing stage, but seven years later, it has blossomed into the most fulfilling passion that I never even knew I had.

Blogging stuck because of all of my amazing readers and fans around the world who actually took the time to read my musings, make my crafts, and cook my recipes. Slowly but surely, their comments and emails began to trickle in — and they fueled my creative fire. I just wanted to keep sharing and creating, so I challenged myself to think outside the box and keep at it. For my thirtieth birthday, my husband surprised me by gifting me with a cooking course at the Center for Kosher Culinary Arts and one day at a time, that teenage girl who used salt instead of sugar in the salad dressing began to look at food in a different way.

When I started to take my food more seriously, I realized that my photography had to follow suit. I knew little about photography and shot everything in automatic mode, but I knew that had to change. I finally mustered up the courage to attend a photography class and switched my camera to manual mode. I bought some photography books, watched YouTube videos in my spare time, and scrutinized the photography on my favorite food blogs. The more I shot, the more I learned and as my photos improved, my passion for bold flavors and spices began to take hold.

I always say that my food blogging journey is a testament to the fact that with hard work and lots of practice — you can do anything! This is all a dream that so many of you have watched evolve into a reality. I'm so thankful to be able to gift my fans and followers with this book — your love, feedback, and support over the years have motivated me to keep going, bigger and brighter than ever before.

One of the best parts about food blogging is being a part of the kosher food blogging community. Having friends whom I can lean on for advice, support, and inspiration is key to my success. I can't thank my foodie friends enough for being there for me all these years!

When it came time for me to write a cookbook, finding a central theme was the hardest part. Over the years, I had come to find my niche in the industry — putting a modern twist on traditional Jewish foods. Don't get me wrong, I still love the comfort foods of my youth. There's really nothing quite like Bubby's stuffed cabbage and matzah ball soup. But times have changed, and the kosher food industry has evolved. Today, kosher food is spicier and bolder than the food we grew up eating. There's an emphasis on fresh and seasonal ingredients, less processed foods, and healthier nondairy alternatives. Modern kosher food reinterprets and reinvents tradition, while still staying true to our heritage. It's food that's influenced by cultural cuisine and not limited to, but inspired by, kosher guidelines. There is still a place for the kosher comfort foods of our youth, and for that there are hundreds of cookbooks. But for now, it's time for *Millennial Kosher*.

Chanie Apfelbaum

How to Cook
MILLENNIAL KOSHER

A Millennial might be defined as a person reaching young adulthood in the early 21st century (and technically speaking, I probably missed the boat on that), but what is the millennial kosher kitchen? The millennial kosher kitchen is one in which food is reinvented and reimagined in new and exciting ways. It includes ingredients that are healthier, fresher, and more vibrant than ever before. Yesterday's margarine is today's coconut oil, bone broth is the new chicken soup, and the onion soup mix of our youth is replaced with umami-rich porcini mushroom powder. The recipes in this book include a combination of modern, cultural, balanced, savory, trendy, colorful, and composed dishes that draw inspiration from the following food philosophies.

EAT IN SEASON

The farm-to-table philosophy has influenced modern cuisine in recent years and is slowly making its way into the kosher industry. Restaurants are serving up seasonal menus and home cooks are signing up for CSA (Community Supported Agriculture) baskets filled with fresh produce from local farms. Eating in season is so beneficial not only because seasonal produce is more flavorful, it is also less expensive and more nutritious. In order to preserve foods that are out of season, produce is often covered in pesticides, waxes, and preservatives to maintain their fresh appearance. Whereas produce harvested at the peak of freshness does not require unnatural preservatives.

FRESH IS BEST

We are so lucky to live in an era of abundance. While our ancestors were scrubbing laundry by hand and making butter from scratch, we have so much available to us! The kosher industry in particular has grown by leaps and bounds, and making from-scratch meals is no longer a necessity. As a mom of five, I am thankful for bottled sauces and other prepared ingredients that make life so much easier, but I'm also mindful of the chemicals, preservatives, and genetically modified ingredients that go into processed food. I'm not above using processed ingredients (matzah ball mix and sweet chili sauce are my guilty pleasures!) but overall, I do believe that fresh is best. I try to use fresh herbs, citrus, and spices most of the time, and when I purchase processed foods, I try to look for items with a short list of ingredients that I can recognize.

COOK WITH COLOR

At my cooking demos and classes, I always joke that all traditional Jewish food is brown. Gefilte fish, golden chicken soup with matzah balls, roast chicken, potato kugel and brisket — all beige and monochrome! People eat with their eyes first, so setting a colorful table is the first step to whetting the appetite of your guests. When I plan out a Shabbos menu, I always think in terms of color: Do I have something orange (squash), green (asparagus), red (roasted tomatoes)? When I build a dish, I think about the garnishes I can use to incorporate pops of color: fresh parsley or pomegranate seeds, microgreens or shaved beets. Garnishes go a long way in adding freshness, color, and flavor both to your individual dishes and to your menu as a whole.

MENUS MATTER

When I was growing up, my mom would make one large salad and maybe a dip or two to serve alongside the fish on Shabbos. Somehow, in today's day and age, kosher cooks have come to serve an elaborate mezze of salads and dips, soups with accompaniments, and several proteins and sides. In this respect, I don't believe bigger is always better. Serving a meal of balanced flavors and dishes that work together is more beneficial in the long run. It's less work (in both prep and clean up!), the food is more enjoyable because the dishes complement each other, and the meal is served with more finesse. I like to think of my meal in terms of a restaurant menu, including appetizers, entrees, and dessert. If you were ordering a meal at a restaurant, you wouldn't order six salads or a few different mains. Choose quality over quantity and build your menu as a composed dish, with mains and side dishes that work together in terms of flavor and presentation.

SPICE THINGS UP

One of the greatest gifts to modern kosher cuisine is the plethora of spices and ethnic foods that have become available on the kosher market. Going out of your comfort zone helps you explore different flavors and ingredients that will keep your food fresh and exciting. On long holidays, with several back-to-back meals, I love to host with a specific cultural theme, such as French, Mexican, or Thai. This keeps your menu focused and your food becomes fun and exciting instead of repetitive and familiar.

COOK SAVORY

In my mother's kitchen, everything was seasoned with a heavy dose of sugar. It was delicious, don't get me wrong, but as I grew up and began to appreciate the savory quality of foods, I realized that sugar just doesn't have a place in certain dishes. I always joke about the salad dressing fiasco from my teenage years, where I used salt instead of sugar in the dressing, but the real humor in that is the fact that we are putting sugar into our salads! Isn't the purpose of a salad to start the meal with a healthy dose of vegetables? Of course, there is place for a bit of sweetener to balance out the acid in a dressing, but sugar usage is often heavy-handed, especially in Ashkenazi cuisine. I'm on a mission to bring savory back! It wasn't easy because my palate was conditioned to sweet foods, but slowly and gradually, I began to reduce the amount of sweetener I added to foods. Instead of adding sugar to salad dressings, I add fresh citrus and herbs or spicy harissa and umami-rich soy sauce to build natural savory flavor.

WHAT IS UMAMI?

Umami is known as the fifth taste. After sweet, salty, sour, and bitter, umami refers to food that is intensely savory. Some natural forms of kosher umami include miso, soy sauce, dried mushrooms, truffles, seaweed, Parmesan cheese, anchovies and kosher beef (or lamb) fry.

LIGHTEN UP

Kosher food has a reputation for being heavy, and rightfully so. There's a reason we all want to take a nap after our Shabbos cholent! Learning to lighten up our menus, our dishes, and even our attitude about food makes the cooking experience so much more enjoyable. With Shabbos dinner every week and so many holidays to cook for, cooking becomes a chore because we take it so seriously. Try to think outside the box and explore different cuisines or veer away from a recipe and make it your own. Putting your own spin on classic dishes will put the fun back into things, and you'll look at food as more than just a means to satiate others, but as an expression of yourself and your creative spirit.

TRACK THE TRENDS

Food trends keep things fresh and exciting in the kitchen, and when we encourage our local purveyors, restaurants, and stores to kosherize trending dishes, it keeps the kosher food world ahead of the curve instead of behind the times.

LEARN THE LINGO

Cooking is an act that incorporates all the senses, from preparing the ingredients to the sounds of the food sizzling in the pan and the aroma of it cooking. Presenting the final dish is a feast for the eyes, culminating in the final act of tasting and enjoying the fruits of your labor. The one thing that is often overlooked is actually giving your dish a name! I love to walk my guests through the menu, explaining what each dish is. Learning the lingo and using the correct culinary terminology can fancy up your dish without any effort. Calling a dip an aioli, a tart a galette, or a meat sauce a bolognese makes it more sophisticated and appealing.

REINTERPRET TRADITION

Some may disagree with me (especially my Bubby!), but I believe there's a place for reinventing our traditions in a modern way while still staying true to our heritage. There will always be a place for chicken soup in the home of every *Yiddishe mammeh*, but putting your own spin on hamantashen, potato latkes, or jelly donuts helps breathe new life into old traditions, keeping them fun and exciting for the next generation.

FIND THE RIGHT BALANCE

Balance is an integral part of cooking. Whether it's balancing the flavors in a dish or balancing the dishes on a menu, consider the big picture. One of my pet peeves is when people serve carbs on carbs for dinner. I'm no nutritionist, and I don't believe in counting calories, but I do believe that every meal should include a protein, a carb, and a vegetable. I've also adopted Meatless Mondays into my meal rotation, because plant-based meals are all the rage and we can all use a break from animal protein after the weekend.

BE RESOURCEFUL

We live in a time when people have become more conscious of food waste than ever before. I have a strong passion for reinventing leftovers and one of my favorite things to do at the end of the week is to empty out my fridge and take stock of all of the unused ingredients. I love to challenge myself to create dishes based on those ingredients, be it a soup, a pizza, or a salad. And as I always say, if all else fails, just roast, roast, roast and #putaneggonit. How's that for *Millennial Kosher*?

The
MILLENNIAL KOSHER KITCHEN

Tools & Equipment

Aside from a well-stocked pantry, having the proper tools is imperative to success in the kitchen. Using the appropriate kitchen tools helps streamline the cooking process, making it much more enjoyable.

TOOLS

- **BASICS**:

  mixing bowls

  liquid measuring cups: such as Pyrex

  dry measuring cups

  measuring spoons

  peelers

  wooden spoons

  turning spatula

  silicone spatulas

  chopsticks: for slicing hasselback recipes

  pastry brush

  whisks

  ziplock or piping bags

  potato masher

  box grater

  rolling pin

  pizza wheel

  can opener

  corkscrew

  salt cellar

  cheesecloth

  colander

  wooden chopping block

  plastic cutting boards: for raw fish, meat, and poultry

  ice cream scoops: for portioning out batter, latkes, meatballs, and matzah balls

- **CHOPPER**: A chopper is not a necessary tool, especially if you know how to use a knife properly, but ever since my husband bought me one as a gift, we love using it to make Israeli salad, which we serve at almost every meal.

- **FLOUR SACK TOWELS**: Thin, white cotton towels are ideal for covering dough, making latkes, removing skins from nuts and chickpeas, drying lettuce, straining stock, and making homemade cheese.

- **FOOD SCALE**: Use to weigh ingredients and portion dough (e.g., so each challah is the same size).

- **KNIVES**: A sharp knife is the most essential tool in the kitchen. Find a knife that you feel comfortable and confident using — it is an extension of your hand. Keep your knives sharpened, using a whetstone or electric sharpener. My must-haves include:

  Santoku knife: *multipurpose Japanese knife with a cleaver-like shape and Granton (dimpled) edge.*

  Chef's knife: *multipurpose knife with a pointed tip*

  Paring knife: *for small jobs such as a peeling and slicing small fruits and vegetables*

  Serrated knife: *for slicing challah, bread, tomatoes, and melons*

  Kitchen shears: *for breaking down poultry, snipping herbs, cutting dough, twine and parchment paper*

- **MANDOLINE**: A mandoline is used to slice fruits and vegetable uniformly, in varying thicknesses. Many mandolines offer different blades, such as julienne blades and french fry blades. I like to use it for slicing potatoes for gratin, beets and other root vegetables for homemade chips, cabbage for coleslaw, and other vegetables to use as garnishes.

- **MICROPLANE**: Use to zest citrus, grate fresh ginger (to me, there's nothing worse than biting into a big piece of ginger!), shallots for dressing, and garlic.

11

- **PLASTIC SQUEEZE BOTTLES**: I keep labeled squeeze bottles of extra virgin olive oil, light olive oil, and canola oil on hand at all times. Also useful for drizzling homemade sauces, spicy mayo, and chocolate.

- **POTS & PANS**: The best advice I can give people about pots and pans is not to buy packaged sets, but rather invest in specific pots. I believe every cook should own:

  stock pot: *for stocks and soup*

  saucepans: *for sauces, rice, grains, hardboiled eggs*

  cast iron skillet: *for recipes that need a good sear; shallow frying*

  Dutch oven: *for roasts and stews*

  nonstick frying pan: *for eggs and zoodles*

  wok: *for stir fries, fried rice, and Asian dishes*

  roasting pans/sheet pans/ rimmed baking sheets: *for roasting proteins, vegetables, and cookies*

  Bundt pan, springform pan, and tart pan: *for baking*

- **JULIENNE PEELER**: A julienne peeler looks just like a regular peeler, except that the blade is separated into small microblades so that when you peel something, you get thin julienne strips instead of a single strip. A julienne peeler is the perfect tool to make quick and easy zucchini noodles (zoodles), carrot strips for soups, and cucumber strips for salad. I prefer the OXO brand.

- **SIEVE, FINE MESH IN DIFFERENT SIZES**: Fine mesh sieves or strainers are used to steam vegetables, cook ramen noodles in soup, squeeze citrus (to catch the pits), and sprinkle powdered sugar.

- **SKIMMER**: Use to skim scum from broths and chicken soup. It can also remove whole spices and herbs from sauces and lift poached eggs, gnocchi, and ravioli from the cooking water.

- **SPIRALIZER**: A spiralizer is a hand-operated machine that creates noodles out of fruits and vegetables. While I typically use a julienne peeler for zoodles, I love to use a spiralizer to make beet noodles, carrot noodles, butternut squash noodles, and even apple noodles. Spiralizing is helpful for those on low carb diets or people who want to add more vegetables into their diet in a fun and creative way.

- **THERMOMETERS**: Oven thermometers ensure proper temperature; using meat thermometers helps you prevent meat and poultry from overcooking; candy thermometers are used in deep frying and candy making.

- **TONGS**: Use to toss pasta, lift hot food off the grill, and remove corn from hot water or fried food from oil. My favorite use for tongs is as a juicer! Simply place half of a lemon or lime between the V of the tongs and press closed.

- **WIRE/COOLING RACK**: Cool cookies, drain fried foods (to keep them from getting soggy), and glaze confections with chocolate on a rack. Use racks when crisping beef fry and "oven frying."

EQUIPMENT

- **BASICS:**

immersion blender	*hand mixer or stand mixer*
food processor	
blender	*crockpot*

- **NON-ESSENTIALS:**

bread machine	*waffle iron*
deep fryer or air fryer	*panini press*

- **IMMERSION CIRCULATOR or SOUS VIDE MACHINE**: *Sous vide* means "under vacuum," and it is a method of cooking vacuum-sealed food in a temperature-controlled water bath for gentle, slow cooking. Sous vide is especially beneficial for cooking meat, because the cooking process tenderizes cheaper cuts and offers superior, even and precise results.

- **INSTAPOT**: A pressure cooker that does the job of several appliances in one, including a slow cooker, rice cooker, and more.

Ingredients

Having a well-stocked fridge and pantry allows you to be creative in the kitchen, make use of leftovers, and prepare balanced meals. I love to experiment with new condiments and spice blends, but these are some of the basics I try to keep on hand.

BASIC

- **OILS:** Some oils perform well at high temperatures; others are best used in salad dressings or over moderate heat.

  avocado oil: *Good for high heat cooking, heart healthy. Moderate avocado flavor.*

  canola oil: *Good for frying and high heat cooking. Flavorless.*

  coconut oil: *Solid at room temperature, making it a great replacement for butter in pareve recipes. For very mild coconut flavor, choose refined coconut oil.*

  extra virgin olive oil: *Good for dressings, as a "finishing" oil for vegetables and proteins, and cooking over moderate heat. Richly flavored.*

  grapeseed oil: *Great for high heat cooking and salad dressings. Flavorless.*

  light olive oil: *Ideal for salad dressings (if you do not like the flavor of heavier olive oil), sautéing, and stir frying.*

  sesame oil: *Add to dressings, marinades, and stir fries. Richly flavored, a little goes a long way.*

  white truffle oil: *Not ideal for cooking, Use as a finishing oil or mixed into mayonnaise.*

- **VINEGARS:**

  apple cider vinegar: *Good for salad dressings, barbecue sauces, and marinades.*

  balsamic vinegar: *Good for salad dressing, roasting vegetables, mixed with olive oil for dipping bread, or reduced to a syrup for appetizers and desserts.*

  distilled white vinegar: *For pickling.*

  red and white wine vinegar: *Good for marinades and salad dressing.*

  rice vinegar: *Sweeter and less acidic than other vinegars. Good for pickling, salad dressings, sushi rice, and Asian recipes.*

- **HOT SAUCES and PASTES:** Hot sauces add flavor and heat to recipes. The type of hot sauce you use depends on the cuisine you are cooking; however, some may be interchangeable.

  gochujang: *Korean fermented red chili paste. Thick and pasty with a richly sweet and spicy flavor. (Available on Amazon from Koko Food.)*

  harissa: *Moroccan/Tunisian chili paste made with seeds and spices. Available in green and red varieties. (Available in Middle Eastern markets and in the ethnic aisle of your grocery store.)*

  Louisiana-style hot sauce: *American hot sauce, vinegary, and thin; add to just about anything.*

  sambal oelek: *Southeast Asian chili paste made with chilies and vinegar. Interchangeable with chili garlic sauce (not to be confused with sweet chili sauce). (Available in the ethnic aisle of your grocery store.)*

  schug: *Yemenite chili paste made with herbs, seeds, and spices. Available in green and red varieties. (Available in Middle Eastern markets and sometimes in the refrigerated section of kosher supermarkets.)*

  sriracha: *Thai thick and creamy hot sauce, moderate with a hint of sweetness. My hot sauce of choice! (Available in the ethnic aisle or near the hot sauces in your grocery store; I prefer the Huy Fong brand.)*

- **UMAMI:** Umami is known as the fifth taste, after sweet, salty, sour, and bitter. Umami refers to food that is intensely savory. The following foods are rich in umami:

  dried mushrooms: *(Available online and in Whole Foods stores.)*

  fish sauce, anchovies, or anchovy paste *(I use Roland brand anchovy paste.)*

  nori/kombu/wakame: *Types of seaweed (available online and in Whole Foods stores).*

kosher beef and lamb "bacon": *Also known as facon and beef fry, this is a cut from the breast or plate that is cured and smoked.*

miso paste: *Fermented soybean paste comes in a range of colors, depending on how long it has aged. I prefer white miso, the youngest and sweetest variety. (Available in most supermarkets, sometimes in the refrigerated section.)*

Parmesan cheese/nutritional yeast *(Available in Whole Foods stores.)*

soy sauce, tamari *(gluten free),* **liquid aminos, coconut aminos** *(soy-free replacement for soy sauce; available in Whole Foods stores).*

OTHER PANTRY ESSENTIALS

- **BAKING POWDER, BAKING SODA**

- **BRANDY, BOURBON, RUM, RED and WHITE WINES**: Never use "cooking wine" from the supermarket; rather, use leftover wine or purchase a less expensive bottle.

- **BROTH:** I love Imagine No-Chicken broth for pareve dishes.

- **CANNED BEANS**:

cannellini	kidney
garbanzo	black
pinto	

- **CANNED TOMATOES, TOMATO SAUCE, TOMATO PASTE, MARINARA SAUCE**

- **COCOA POWDER, DUTCH PROCESS COCOA POWDER**

- **COCONUT MILK:** Canned, full-fat and light *(I prefer the Roland brand).*

- **MUSTARD**

Dijon	spicy deli
whole grain	yellow

- **DRIED FRUIT**

apricots	raisins
prunes	dates
cranberries	cherries

- **FLOURS**

all-purpose flour	white whole wheat flour
high gluten flour	almond flour

- **GOOD-QUALITY CHOCOLATE CHIPS:** I love California Gourmet.

- **GRAINS**

quinoa	wheat berries
wild rice	bulgur
farro	barley
freekeh	oats

- **INSTANT ESPRESSO:** I love Café Bustelo.

- **JAMS**

apricot	cherry
strawberry	fig

- **KETCHUP**

- **LIQUID SMOKE:** Provides smoky flavor without the grill. *(Available in most major supermarkets near the barbecue sauces.)*

- **MARZIPAN, ALMOND PASTE** *(Available in most major supermarkets in the baking aisle.)*

- **MAYONNAISE:** I prefer canola or olive oil mayonnaise.

- **MIRIN:** Rice cooking wine. *(Available in most supermarkets near the Asian ingredients or vinegars.)*

- **NONSTICK COOKING SPRAY**

canola oil	coconut oil
olive oil	with flour for baking

- **NUTS:**

almonds	pecans
cashews	pine nuts
chestnuts	pistachios
hazelnuts	walnuts
peanuts	

- **PANKO CRUMBS, BREADCRUMBS, CORNFLAKE CRUMBS, MATZAH MEAL**

- **COUSCOUS, PASTA, RAMEN NOODLES**

- **PICKLES, OLIVES,** and **CAPERS**

- **POMEGRANATE MOLASSES:** Concentrated pomegranate syrup. *(Available online and in Middle Eastern markets.)*

- **SEEDS**

chia seeds	*pumpkin seeds*
flax seeds	*sesame seeds (black and white)*
hemp seeds	*sunflower seeds*
poppy seeds	

- **SILAN** (date honey)**, HONEY, MAPLE SYRUP**

- **SUGARS:**

confectioner's	*demerara*
dark brown	*granulated*

- **SUNDRIED TOMATOES**

- **SWEET CHILI SAUCE**

- **TAHINI PASTE**

- **TAMARIND PASTE:** Sour paste from tamarind fruit. *(Available online and in Middle Eastern markets.)*

- **VANILLA and ALMOND EXTRACTS**

SPICES

You should be able to find most of these in major supermarkets, specialty spices can be found online or in Whole Foods markets or Trader Joe's. Israeli spice blends are available from Pereg or at Middle Eastern markets.

- **CHILIES & PEPPERS**

black peppercorns	*chipotle chili powder*
pink peppercorns	*allepo chili flakes*
crushed red pepper flakes	*urfa biber chili flakes*
cayenne pepper	*gochugaru (Korean chili flakes)*
ancho chili powder	

- **SALT**

kosher salt	*sea salt*
Maldon salt	*seasoned salt*
pink Himalayan salt	*truffle salt*

- **SPICE BLENDS**

baharat	*Montreal steak seasoning*
dukkah (nut and seed blend)	*Old Bay seasoning*
everything bagel mix	*poultry seasoning*
garam masala	*ras el hanout*
hawaj	*shawarma spice*
herbes de Provence	*za'atar*

- **SPICES**

allspice	*nutmeg*
basil	*onion powder and flakes*
bay leaves	*oregano*
cardamom	*parsley*
cinnamon	*rosemary*
cloves	*smoked paprika*
coriander	*sage*
cumin	*sumac*
curry	*sweet paprika*
garlic powder and flakes	*thyme*
ginger	*turmeric*
mustard	

FRIDGE

- **BUTTER**

- **CHEESES**

Mozzarella (fresh and shredded)	*ricotta*
	cream
cheddar	*Parmesan*

- **COLD BREW COFFEE**

- **CORN TORTILLAS**

- **EGGS**

- **FRUITS** and **VEGETABLES** (depending on the season)

- **GREEK YOGURT, SOUR CREAM**

- **HERBS,** and **SPICES**

basil	*fresh turmeric*
cilantro	*parsley*
dill	*rosemary*
fresh ginger	*thyme*

- **LEMONS, LIMES**

- **PRESERVED LEMONS** (recipe, page 20)

- **QUICK PICKLED ONIONS** (recipe, page 22)

- **TEMPEH, TOFU, SOY CRUMBLES** *(Available in Whole Foods markets, Trader Joe's, major supermarkets.)*

- **WHOLE MILK, HALF AND HALF, ALMOND MILK**

FREEZER

- **BEEF FRY, PASTRAMI, HOT DOGS, SAUSAGES, SMOKED TURKEY LEGS**

- **GROUND BEEF AND GROUND TURKEY:** I like to freeze it lightly pressed flat in a ziplock bag for easier thawing.

- **CHICKEN** and **BEEF BONES:** for stock and soup.

- **CHICKEN BREASTS:** I like to remove the tenders and freeze them in a separate bag to be used for schnitzel strips.

- **GINGER** and **LEMONGRASS**

- **EDAMAME:** whole and shelled

- **FRUITS AND VEGETABLES**

- **PIZZA DOUGH**

- **PUFF PASTRY, MALAWACH DOUGH, PHYLLO DOUGH**

- **WONTON WRAPPERS**

- **SURIMI MOCK CRAB STICKS**

UNREFRIGERATED PRODUCE

- **BANANAS**

- **GARLIC**

- **ORGANIC SWEET POTATOES**

- **PLANTAINS**

- **RED ONIONS**

- **RUSSET (IDAHO) POTATOES**

- **SHALLOTS**

- **SPANISH ONIONS**

- **TOMATOES**

Notes & Tips

NOTES

- **Oils**: All recipes in this book use **refined** coconut oil or extra virgin olive oil, unless otherwise specified.

- **Eggs**: All recipes in this book use extra large eggs unless otherwise specified.

- **Salt and Pepper**: All recipes in this book use kosher salt and freshly ground black pepper unless otherwise specified.

TIPS

- **How to toast nuts:** Preheat oven to 350°F. Spread nuts in an even layer on a baking sheet. Roast for 8-12 minutes, stirring halfway through, until nuts are fragrant and start to darken in color.

- **How to toast sesame seeds:** Preheat oven to 350°F. Spread sesame seeds in an even layer on a baking sheet. Roast for 10 minutes, stirring halfway through, until seeds are golden and fragrant.

STAPLES

Preserved Lemons

Quick Pickled Onions

Smoked Paprika Croutons

Tahini Two Ways

Fire-Roasted Grape Tomatoes

House Rub

One-Bowl Honey Challah

Crockpot Bone Broth

Spinach Pistachio Pesto

Roasted Eggplant "Boats"

Preserved LEMONS

PAREVE • YIELDS 1 QUART

Preserved lemons are a fairly recent addition to my repertoire. I used to buy them occasionally, for their pungent salty and citrusy punch, but when I started spending my summers in Upstate New York, I'd take advantage of the abundance of Meyer lemons at the local market and prepare a few jars to get through the winter. Don't be intimidated; they are super easy to make, and a little goes a long way in brightening up a dish.

8-10 lemons, Meyer preferred
- kosher salt
- fresh-squeezed lemon juice, as needed

1. Scrub lemons well. Prepare a quart-sized wide-mouth Mason jar, washing well with hot water.

2. Without cutting through to the bottom, cut each lemon into quarters. Spread open the lemon quarters, keeping them attached at the base. Press kosher salt between the quarters, filling the space between them as well.

3. Add about 3 tablespoons kosher salt to the jar. Place the lemons into the jar, pushing down on them and squeezing in as many lemons as possible. The lemons should be completely submerged in the juice that is pressed out of them. If you can't squeeze enough juice out of them, add fresh-squeezed lemon juice to the jar until the lemons are covered. Add more salt; seal the jar.

4. Let the jar sit at room temperature for one week. Every other day, turn it upside down and shake it to distribute the salt and liquids.

5. Put the jar into the refrigerator; turn it upside down every now and then.

6. The lemons will be ready when the rinds have softened, about 4 weeks.

7. To use the lemons, rinse thoroughly to remove excess salt. Discard seeds. Puree a whole lemon to add to dishes, or finely dice the peel. You can also crush the peel with a garlic crusher.

8. Store the lemons in the refrigerator for 6-8 months.

NOTE

Before adding the lemons to the jar, you can also add dried chilies or spices, such as cinnamon sticks, bay leaves, coriander seeds, cloves, and peppercorns.

USES

Add preserved lemon to salad dressings, marinades, braised chicken, meat, or fish.

Quick
PICKLED ONIONS

PAREVE ▪ YIELDS 1-2 CUPS

There's just something about pickled onions. They're crunchy. Sweet. Sour. Beautiful. And yes, even quick and easy. It's amazing how just a small forkful of pickled onions will elevate a dish, and once you start, you'll never go back. I always have a jar of these in the fridge.

½ cup	rice vinegar
½ cup	water
¼ cup	sugar
1½ tsp	kosher salt
1 small	red onion, sliced into thin half-moons

NOTE

You can also use this brine over sliced cucumbers for instant pickles or other veggies of your choice.

USES

Pickled onions make a great addition to fish tacos, pulled beef sandwiches, hot dogs, grilled cheese, burgers, and salads.

1. In a 1-quart pot, bring vinegar, water, sugar, and salt to a boil. Remove from heat. Add onion; set aside to cool.

2. Add cooled onion and pickling liquid to a 16-ounce jar; refrigerate for up to 1 month.

Smoked Paprika
CROUTONS

PAREVE ▪ YIELDS 4 CUPS

Artisan breads have recently become popularized in the kosher food market, and with sourdough so readily available, we've turned into sourdough snobs. Once we took the sourdough plunge, it was so hard to go back to traditional bread, so I decided to learn to make it myself. Chaya Suri Leitner of @spiceandzest taught me everything I needed to know, and although I've never been much of a baker, I enjoy the challenge. I still kill my starter every few months and have to resort to store-bought varieties, but they are good enough for my family and even better when you use the leftovers for croutons. The only problem with these is that they never quite make it to the salad, because we eat them all right out of the pan!

10 oz.	day-old sourdough bread (about ½ loaf)
1 Tbsp	smoked paprika
½ tsp	kosher salt
3 Tbsp	olive oil

1. Preheat oven to 350°F.

2. Cut bread into 1-inch cubes; spread on a baking sheet. Sprinkle with smoked paprika and salt; drizzle with olive oil. Toss cubes with your hands to distribute oil and spices. Spread into a single layer.

3. Bake for 10-20 minutes, stirring once, until toasted and crispy.

NOTE

Baking times vary, depending on the age and hydration of the bread. If your bread is very moist, leave it on the counter to dry for a few hours after cutting it. Adjust baking times, as needed, until croutons are crispy.

VARIATION

For rustic croutons, tear the bread into pieces instead of slicing.

Tahini
TWO WAYS

PAREVE · YIELDS ¾ CUP EACH

Preparing tahini is an essential part of my Sunday fridge stock. We put it on everything from salad, to eggplant, potatoes, and eggs. I use it as a grab-and-go dip for veggies, and I love that I can adapt it by adding different flavors for a fun twist.

CLASSIC TAHINI

½ cup	tahini paste
1 Tbsp	chopped parsley
1 clove	garlic, minced
·	juice of ½ lemon
¼ tsp	cumin
⅓ cup	ice water
·	salt, to taste

OPTIONAL TOPPINGS

- olive oil, paprika, white sesame seeds, lemon slices

1. Stir tahini paste thoroughly before measuring, as oil and solids tend to separate.

2. In a bowl, mix tahini paste, parsley, garlic, lemon juice, and cumin. Add ½ cup ice water; whisk until emulsified. If you prefer a thinner tahini, add more water until desired consistency is reached. Season with salt, to taste.

ASIAN TAHINI DRESSING

½ cup	tahini paste
2 Tbsp	lime juice
1 Tbsp	soy sauce
1 large clove	garlic, minced
1 tsp	grated fresh ginger
1 tsp	sriracha
⅓ cup	ice water
·	salt, to taste

OPTIONAL TOPPINGS

- toasted sesame oil, sriracha, black sesame seeds, lime slices

1. Stir tahini paste thoroughly before measuring, as oil and solids tend to separate.

2. In a bowl, combine tahini paste, lime juice, soy sauce, garlic, ginger, and sriracha. Slowly add water, whisking until smooth and emulsified. Season with salt, to taste.

--- TIP ---

To use tahini as a dip, use a bit less water; to use tahini as a dressing, use a bit more water.

--- VARIATION ---

For those with sesame allergies or for Pesach use, replace tahini with almond butter. For a Sweet Tahini Dip, see recipe on page 50.

--- USES ---

Serve with Israeli Salad, shawarma chicken, fresh pita, malawach, roasted eggplant, and more!

--- USES ---

Drizzle over spiralized cucumbers and serve with sliced scallions and toasted sesame seeds; use as a dressing for chicken salad, or serve as a dip for broccoli or cauliflower.

Fire-Roasted
GRAPE TOMATOES

PAREVE ▪ YIELDS 2 CUPS

In my house, we buy pints and pints of grape tomatoes for sweet and crunchy snacking, salads, and crudité platters, but inevitably, there are always some left over at the end of the week. I never like to waste ingredients, so I turn them into a sweet and smoky condiment that elevates sandwiches and pairs well with fish, meat, and poultry. It's amazing to see how you can turn slightly shriveled tomatoes into something extraordinary with a little effort and just a few basic ingredients.

2 pints	grape tomatoes
2 Tbsp	grapeseed or avocado oil
2 Tbsp	balsamic vinegar
▪	salt, to taste
▪	pepper, to taste

1. Preheat broiler to high.

2. Place all ingredients onto a baking sheet; broil on high for 10-15 minutes (depending on how soft the tomatoes are), shaking the baking sheet every few minutes.

3. Store in an airtight container for up to one week.

— USES —

Roasted grape tomatoes make a great topping for soup, crostini, pizza, pasta, and sandwiches.

HOUSE RUB

PAREVE • YIELDS APPROXIMATELY 6 TABLESPOONS

You know how some people collect shot glasses or salt and pepper shakers? I collect spices. A peek through my spice cabinet will take you on a tour of international flavors and culinary exploration. From flavored salts (of varying coarseness, of course) to assorted chili peppers and spice blends, spices add color, texture, flavor, and heat to food. I love to play around with different blends, and this pastrami-inspired mix has become a kitchen staple.

2 Tbsp	coriander
1 tsp	coarsely ground black pepper
1 tsp	granulated garlic
1 tsp	onion powder
1 Tbsp	brown sugar
2 tsp	mustard powder
1 Tbsp	smoked paprika
1½ tsp	kosher salt

- In a small bowl, combine all ingredients. Store in an airtight container for up to six months.

NOTE

Granulated garlic is less finely ground than garlic powder, but you can use garlic powder instead if you can't find granulated garlic.

USES

This all-purpose rub works great on brisket, grilled chicken breasts, whole roasted chicken (see page 150), salmon, and fish tacos.

One-Bowl
HONEY CHALLAH

PAREVE • YIELDS 6 LARGE OR 8 MEDIUM CHALLAHS • FREEZER FRIENDLY

I was never really much of a challah person — I mean, eating it, yes, but baking it? Not so much. I found the whole challah baking process too messy and time consuming, and since I love to play around in the kitchen on Fridays, there just wasn't enough time to bake AND cook. When I started getting requests to host challah bakes around town, I decided to streamline my challah baking process to make it more doable. This one-bowl wonder, based on my sister-in-law Ruti's recipe, has become my go-to. I line my counter with a plastic tablecloth to keep things clean and even though I have a Magic Mill, I find that making the challah by hand is quicker, easier, and infinitely more delicious.

4 packets	rapid rise yeast (3 Tbsp)
4 cups	warm water, divided
2 Tbsp	sugar
1¼ cups	canola oil
1½ cups	honey
1	egg
2 Tbsp	kosher salt
5 lbs.	high gluten flour
3 Tbsp	canola oil
1	egg + 1 egg yolk, beaten
•	toppings such as everything seasoning, sesame seeds, za'atar, poppy seeds, Sweet Crumbs (see page 274)

1. Bring all ingredients to room temperature. Place yeast, 1 cup warm water, and sugar into a large mixing bowl; stir gently with a spoon. Allow the yeast to sit for a few minutes to bloom.

2. Add oil, honey, egg, salt, and remaining 3 cups warm water; stir to combine.

3. Add half the flour, sifting lightly through your fingers as you pour. Stir mixture with a spoon until creamy.

4. Gradually add most of the remaining flour, mixing with your hands until flour is incorporated. Knead the dough, folding the dough onto itself and turning continuously for 10 minutes, adding more flour, as needed, until the dough is smooth and elastic.

5. Rub dough with oil; cover with a dish towel. Set aside in a warm place to rise until it has doubled in size (1½-2 hours). If you have time, punch down the dough and allow to rise a second time.

6. Divide dough into equal portions; braid as desired. Allow braided loaves to rise for an additional 45 minutes. Brush loaves with beaten egg; add toppings, if desired.

7. While the dough is rising, preheat oven to 350°F. Bake until golden brown, 30-45 minutes. (Challah should sound hollow when the bottom is tapped.) Remove to a rack to cool.

— NOTE —

Challah can be frozen after braiding or after baking.

Crockpot
BONE BROTH

MEAT ▪ YIELDS APPROXIMATELY 11 CUPS ▪ FREEZER FRIENDLY

*If you've ever been sick, chances are Dr. Mom has prescribed some Jewish penicillin —
a hot bowl of chicken soup to make you feel better. As it turns out, "Mom is always right,"
especially if she puts chicken feet in her soup. Chicken feet are high in collagen, which is
what gives the soup its gelatinous jiggle, and it's also what makes bone broth the new soup
for the Millennial soul. Bone broth is a highly nutritious stock made by simmering collagen-
rich animal bones for many hours to draw out their vitamins, minerals, and protein.*

2 lbs.	marrow bones
2 lbs.	knee bones
2	carrots, cut into thirds
2 stalks	celery, cut into thirds
1	onion, cut into wedges
3 cloves	garlic, unpeeled
2 Tbsp	apple cider vinegar
1	bay leaf
12 cups	water

1. Preheat oven to 450°F. Place bones, carrots, celery, onion, and garlic on a baking sheet. You do not need to peel the vegetables. Roast for 45 minutes, until browned.

2. Add bones and vegetables to a crockpot with drippings and bits from the baking sheet. Add vinegar, bay leaf and water. Cook on low for 24 hours.

3. Strain the broth through a fine mesh strainer. Discard solids. Cool; refrigerate overnight. Remove and discard the layer of fat that rose to the top of the broth. The broth should be the consistency of jello; it will liquefy when heated.

4. Divide broth between 1-2-pound containers. Refrigerate for one week or freeze for up to three months. You can also freeze smaller portions in a muffin tin or ice cube tray.

NOTE

You may also use a combination of beef and chicken joint bones that are high in collagen, such as necks and feet from chicken or oxtail and knuckle bones from beef.

USES

You may drink the broth on its own, adding salt and pepper to taste, or use as a base for ramen soup, gravy, or in place of beef broth. You can also add small quantities to mashed potatoes, baby food, and sauces.

Spinach Pistachio
PESTO

DAIRY OR PAREVE • YIELDS APPROXIMATELY 1¼ CUPS • FREEZER FRIENDLY

I love a good pesto. What I don't love is washing the sand off my basil, burning my expensive pine nuts by mistake, and then having the pesto turn black before I even finish making it! I was determined to simplify the process, so I subbed in baby spinach for the basil and pistachios for the pine nuts. Not only is the combination so buttery and fresh, but the spinach keeps it beautifully bright green, even after days in the fridge.

3 cups	(packed) baby spinach
⅔ cup	toasted unsalted pistachios
1 large or 2 small	cloves garlic
2 tsp	lemon juice, plus more to taste
¼-½ cup	olive oil
•	salt, to taste
•	pepper, to taste
½ cup	grated Parmesan cheese, optional, for dairy meals

1. In a food processor, pulse spinach, garlic, pistachios, lemon juice, and Parmesan cheese (if using) until finely minced. While the processor is running, slowly drizzle olive oil through the feeding tube until all the ingredients are pureed, scraping down the sides of the bowl as necessary.

2. Season with salt, pepper, and additional lemon juice, to taste.

VARIATION

This formula works for many types of greens and nuts, so make your own variations! You can use fresh leafy greens such as basil, parsley, kale, arugula, or beet greens and nuts such as almonds, hazelnuts, walnuts, macadamia nuts, and pine nuts.

TIP

Freeze in ice-cube trays for ease of use .

NOTES

You can add more or less olive oil, depending on the consistency you want. I like to start off with thicker pesto and add olive oil as needed, depending on what I am using it for (thinner for sauces, thicker for spreads).

I prefer to use unsalted pistachios so I can better control the pesto's salt content, but if you cannot find them, you may use salted, or buy raw pistachios and toast them as per the method on page 17.

Roasted Eggplant "BOATS"

PAREVE · YIELDS 2 SERVINGS · FREEZER FRIENDLY

I'm not the most enthusiastic salad person. I mean, I like a good salad, don't get me wrong, but I just don't want to be eating salad every day. I need alternatives. Roasted eggplant boats are the fridge-stock staple that gets me through the week without relying on bread and other carbs to fill me up. I usually prep two eggplants on Sunday, to fill with everything from shakshuka to cheese, chicken, or falafel. If there's any left over at the end of the week, I just mix it with some tahini for an easy babaganoush.

1	eggplant, unpeeled, halved lengthwise
2 Tbsp	grapeseed or other high heat cooking oil
·	salt, to taste
·	freshly squeezed lemon juice, optional

1. Preheat broiler to high.

2. Brush eggplant halves with oil on all sides. Place flesh-side down on a baking sheet; season eggplant skin with salt; broil for 20-25 minutes, until skin is charred and flesh is soft.

3. Before serving, use a fork to lightly break up eggplant flesh; season with salt and freshly squeezed lemon juice (optional).

NOTE

Do not line baking sheet with parchment paper, as it can catch fire under the broiler.

USES

Serve the eggplant boats with a drizzle of tahini, top with shawarma, salad, or falafel (page 200). You can also add marinara and cheese for a low-carb eggplant Parmesan — or make Lamb Moussaka Eggplant "Boats" (page 192).

Marble Cake   350°

9 eggs   1 hr.
2 c Sugar
2 c flour
1 vanilla
1 Marg. stick
1/2 cup sugar
4 lbs. cocoa
4 Tbs. water
2 tbs. coffee
1 lemon with peel

(over)

Quick Marble
2 cups sugar Cake   325%
1 cup oil   50 min
3 teas. B.P.
4 eggs added

1 cup cold water Alternate
3 cups flour
2 teas vanilla
3 Heaping Cocoa - 1/2 batter

BREAKFAST & BRUNCH

Marble Cake Pancakes

Ramen Shakshuka

World's Best Corn Muffins

Cookie Butter Frappuccino

Sweet & Savory Toast

Peanut Butter Granola

Malawach Egg-in-a-Hole

Breakfast Sachlav

Overnight Oats Affogato

Green, Eggs & Latke

Marble Cake
PANCAKES

DAIRY ▪ YIELDS 8-10 PANCAKES

Marble cake is one of those foods that remind me of my youth. There was always a tray of it at the kiddush on Shabbos, and if we were lucky, my mom would make it from scratch, swirling the chocolate into the pound cake just so. In my house, kokosh cake is the cake of choice on Shabbos mornings, but during the week we eat our marble cake in pancake form, and, dare I say, it's even better than the cake version.

2 cups	all-purpose flour
1 Tbsp	baking powder
½ tsp	kosher salt
⅓ cup	sugar
2	eggs
1¾ cup	milk
1 tsp	vanilla
¼ cup	melted butter or oil
1 Tbsp	cocoa powder
▪	butter or oil, for greasing the pan
▪	butter, for serving
▪	maple syrup, for serving

1. In a mixing bowl, whisk together flour, baking powder, salt, and sugar. In a separate bowl, whisk together eggs, milk, vanilla, and melted butter or oil. Add the wet ingredients to the dry; stir to combine. Don't overmix the batter.

2. Remove ½-cup batter to a small bowl; mix the cocoa powder into it.

3. Grease a nonstick pan or griddle; heat over medium heat. Pour about ⅓ cup batter onto griddle. Working quickly, add 3 small dollops of cocoa batter onto the pancakes; swirl with the flat point of a skewer or the tip of a knife to create a marbled effect.

4. When bubbles start to appear, flip the pancake over and cook until lightly browned. Repeat with remaining batters.

5. Serve with butter and maple syrup.

Ramen
SHAKSHUKA

PAREVE ▪ YIELDS 3 SERVINGS

Ah, shakshuka, you are my all-time favorite breakfast. I love changing you up with different ingredients, and serving you for brunch, placing the pan right in the middle of the table, family style. I've created so many variations of shakshuka on my blog over the years — from garbanzo bean shakshuka to spaghetti squash shakshuka, eggplant shakshuka, and even Mexican quinoa shakshuka. This ramen-based recipe is a super-simplified version, so you can make it with very few ingredients on hand.

2 cups	marinara sauce
1 tsp	sriracha
1½ cups	water
2 (3-oz.) pkgs	ramen noodles, flavoring packets discarded
6	eggs
2	scallions, sliced
1 tsp	toasted sesame seeds

1. In a skillet, bring marinara sauce, sriracha, and water to a simmer. Add ramen noodles; cook until noodles start to soften, about 2 minutes. Flip noodles; continue to cook until the block of ramen loosens, another 2 minutes. (Don't worry if they are not cooked through; they will continue to cook along with the eggs.)

2. With a spoon, make a well in the sauce. Crack an egg into a small bowl; gently slide it into the well. Repeat, one by one, making wells and sliding in remaining eggs. Cover the skillet; cook until egg whites are set, 4-5 minutes. Garnish with scallions and sesame seeds. Serve immediately.

World's Best CORN MUFFINS

DAIRY OR PAREVE ▪ YIELDS 15 MUFFINS ▪ FREEZER FRIENDLY

*I don't call these world's best corn muffins for nothing.
Make them and see for yourself. You're welcome.*

1½ cups	flour
1½ cups	cornmeal
½ cup	sugar
2 tsp	baking powder
½ tsp	baking soda
½ tsp	kosher salt
1 cup	coconut milk (see Note)
½ cup	canola oil
1	egg
1 (14.75-oz.) can	creamed corn

1. Preheat oven to 350°F. Line a cupcake pan with paper liners or coat with nonstick cooking spray.

2. In a bowl, whisk together flour, cornmeal, sugar, baking powder, baking soda, and salt. In a separate bowl, whisk together milk, oil, and egg. Pour the wet ingredients into the dry ingredients; stir to incorporate. Add the creamed corn; mix to combine.

3. Fill muffin cups ¾-full. Bake for 20-25 minutes until a toothpick inserted comes out clean.

NOTES

I use shelf-stable coconut milk from a carton, but you may use any type of milk in this recipe.

Muffins will stay fresh at room temperature for up to 2 days and will keep for an additional week if refrigerated.

VARIATION

You can also bake this batter in a large loaf pan or a cast-iron skillet.

JALAPEÑO HONEY BUTTER

DAIRY ▪ YIELDS ½ CUP

½ cup (1 stick)	butter
2 Tbsp	honey
1 small	jalapeño, veins and seeds removed, finely diced
½ tsp	kosher salt

1. Bring butter to room temperature. Whip butter with a hand blender; stir in honey, jalapeño, and salt.

2. Spread butter onto a sheet of parchment paper; roll it into a log, twisting the sides of the paper to tighten. Refrigerate until ready to use.

Cookie Butter
FRAPPUCCINO

DAIRY · YIELDS 2 SMALL OR 1 LARGE SERVING

Ah, cookie butter. Where have you been all my life?! Well, apparently, in Belgium. But when local markets started importing the Israeli-made version, the kosher world was hooked. Cookie butter a.k.a. Lotus spread a.k.a. speculoos a.k.a. the best stuff on earth is made by churning spiced biscuits into a creamy peanut-butter-like spread. It needs nothing more than a spoon for eating, but if you really want to take things over the top, try it swirled into cheesecake, ice cream, or in this indulgent frappuccino.

1 Tbsp	instant espresso or strong coffee granules
2 heaping Tbsp	cookie butter, plus more for drizzling
1 Tbsp	maple syrup
1 cup	whole milk
1 cup	ice
▪	whipped cream, optional
▪	Lotus cookies, crushed, optional garnish

1. Place espresso, cookie butter, maple syrup, milk, and ice into a blender; blend until smooth.

2. Melt some cookie butter in the microwave or a small saucepan; drizzle around the inside of the serving glass.

3. Pour blended coffee into the glass; top with whipped cream and crushed Lotus cookies, if desired.

Sweet & Savory
TOAST

When toast became a popular food trend, I took a new interest in breakfast. Pile anything on top of a piece of toasted sourdough and I'll see you at the table.

SWEET TAHINI TOAST
PAREVE

¼ cup	tahini paste, plus more for drizzling
2 Tbsp	silan or honey, plus more for drizzling
1 Tbsp	water
¼ tsp	cinnamon
½ tsp	vanilla
pinch	sea salt
2 slices	cinnamon raisin Ezekiel bread, toasted
•	sesame seeds, for sprinkling
•	crumbled halva, optional

1. Place tahini, silan, water, cinnamon, vanilla, and sea salt into a bowl; whisk until emulsified.

2. Spread tahini mixture over the toast; drizzle with additional tahini. Sprinkle with sesame seeds.

3. Drizzle the toasts lightly with silan; garnish with crumbled halva, if desired.

GREEK AVOCADO TOAST
DAIRY

1	ripe avocado
1 tsp	freshly squeezed lemon juice
•	salt, to taste
2 slices	sourdough bread, toasted
2 slices	tomato
1 small	cucumber, peeled into ribbons
¼ cup	feta cheese crumbles
handful	Kalamata olives
pinch	dried oregano
•	good-quality olive oil, for finishing

1. In a small bowl, mash avocado with lemon and salt.

2. Spread avocado over toast; top with tomato slices, cucumber ribbons, feta, olives, and oregano. Finish with a drizzle of olive oil.

Peanut Butter
GRANOLA

PAREVE • YIELDS APPROXIMATELY 3 CUPS • FREEZER FRIENDLY

I was never really much of a smoothie person, because I prefer to eat my calories instead of drinking them. Then, the smoothie bowl trend introduced me to a whole new way of looking at the blended drink, and now I pile on the toppings and enjoy it with a spoon.

¼ cup	natural peanut butter
¼ cup	maple syrup
2 Tbsp	dark brown sugar
1 Tbsp	peanut, coconut, or canola oil
½ tsp	kosher salt
2 cups	old-fashioned oats
½ cup	honey roasted peanuts, optional

1. Preheat oven to 300°F. Line a baking sheet with parchment paper; set aside.

2. In a small saucepan, combine peanut butter, maple syrup, brown sugar, oil, and salt. Stir over low heat until melted.

3. Place oats into a large bowl. Pour peanut butter mixture over oats; mix to incorporate. Spread mixture onto prepared baking sheet. Bake for 25 minutes, stirring halfway through.

4. Cool completely; add honey roasted peanuts, if desired. Store in an airtight container for up to 1 month.

PB&J SMOOTHIE BOWL

DAIRY OR PAREVE • YIELDS 1 SERVING

1 cup	frozen strawberries or mixed berries
⅓ cup	milk OR any nondairy milk
•	honey or sweetener of choice, to taste (depending on sweetness of fruit)
1 Tbsp	natural peanut butter
1 Tbsp	good quality jam
1 tsp	chia seeds
1 tsp	hemp seeds
2 Tbsp	Peanut Butter Granola

• Blend strawberries, milk, and sweetener (if using) in a blender until creamy. For a thicker smoothie, use less milk; for a thinner smoothie, use more milk. Pour smoothie into a bowl; top with remaining ingredients.

BANANA NUT YOGURT BOWL

DAIRY • YIELDS 1 SERVING

1 (single-serve) container	plain Greek yogurt
1	banana, sliced
2	Medjool dates, chopped
1 Tbsp	peanut butter
2 Tbsp	Peanut Butter Granola
2 tsp	silan or honey
pinch	cinnamon

• Place yogurt into a bowl. Top with sliced banana, dates, peanut butter, granola, honey, and cinnamon.

Malawach
EGG-IN-A-HOLE

DAIRY OR PAREVE • YIELDS 1 SERVING

Malawach is the Yemenite answer to puff pastry. When fried, the malawach puffs up into the crispiest pancake that is heavenly when dipped into freshly ground tomatoes and schug; kid-friendly when topped with pizza sauce and cheese; and all-out indulgent when covered with more butter and honey. Here, I've Millennialized (yes, that's a word now) the classic egg-in-a-hole by using malawach in place of the bread for a dish worthy of Sunday brunch.

1	plum tomato
2 tsp	butter or olive oil
1 disc	frozen malawach dough
1	egg
▪	salt, to taste
▪	prepared schug (recipe follows) OR green harissa, for serving

1. Using a handheld grater, grate the tomato. Season, to taste, with salt. Set aside.

2. Partially thaw malawach. Using a glass or round cookie cutter, cut a hole in the center of the malawach. Set the cut-out dough aside. Heat butter in a nonstick skillet; add malawach. Cook over medium heat until browned and crispy, 3-4 minutes; flip malawach. Pour an egg into the hole in the malawach; cover pan. Cook for 4 minutes, or until egg is set and malawach is crispy. Remove from the pan.

3. Add the cut round to the pan; fry on each side until crispy. Serve fried round with the malawach, grated tomato, and schug.

— VARIATION —

You can also top with crumbled feta, grated cheese, or tahini.

— NOTE —

You can control the heat of the schug by the amount of jalapeño veins and seeds you use. For a mild schug, remove all jalapeno veins and seeds. For a spicier kick, add a little at a time until desired spice level is reached.

SCHUG

PAREVE • YIELDS 1 HEAPING CUP

3	jalapeño peppers
1 large bunch	fresh parsley and/or cilantro (2-3 cups, packed)
4 cloves	garlic
1 tsp	cumin
¼ cup	olive oil
▪	juice of ½ lemon
▪	salt, to taste

▪ Add ingredients to a blender or food processor; puree until smooth.

Breakfast
SACHLAV

DAIRY ▪ YIELDS 2 SERVINGS

My first taste of sachlav was at the Israeli restaurant Bissile, where I used to chill with friends till the wee hours of the morning, eating ftut (chopped malawach dough with cheese and veggies) and chatting with strangers who, by the end of the night, had become friends. The Israelis were always ordering a hot milky drink served in paper cups and I finally mustered up the courage to try it. I didn't know what to think of the rosewater-scented custard, topped with cinnamon, coconut, and walnuts, but I knew I wanted more. Each time I went to Bissile, I'd order it again, not really knowing what it was that I was drinking, but liking it more and more with each cup. Here, I've turned this Israeli classic into an easy breakfast dish — no cornstarch or thickener required.

1½ cups	milk
1 Tbsp	sugar or sweetener, or to taste
pinch	sea salt
3 Tbsp	farina
½ tsp	rosewater
▪	shredded coconut, chopped walnuts, and cinnamon, for serving

1. Add milk to a saucepan; bring to a gentle simmer over low heat.

2. Add sugar and salt; stir to dissolve.

3. Slowly add farina, whisking continuously, until thickened, 3-5 minutes. Stir in the rosewater.

4. Top with coconut, walnuts, and cinnamon. Serve immediately.

— NOTES —

To make this pareve, use any nondairy milk of your choice.

If you don't like the flavor of rosewater, use vanilla extract instead.

Overnight Oats
AFFOGATO

DAIRY · YIELDS 1 SERVING

Overnight oats have become the breakfast of choice for people on the go. You fill a jar with oats, milk, and seasonings of your choice, stick it in the fridge, and voila — a grab-and-go breakfast is ready for the taking the very next morning. I'd never really tried a version that I liked, until one day, I accidentally spilled my coffee into my overnight oats, and the Overnight Oats Affogato was born. Affogato is an Italian specialty in which hot espresso is poured over a scoop of cold ice cream. The ice cream melts into the coffee for a decadent after-dinner drink. Here, I pour my espresso over my overnight oats for a similar effect and get breakfast and coffee in one. I call that a win-win!

½ cup	old-fashioned oats
¾ cup	milk
pinch	salt
pinch	cinnamon, optional
1 Tbsp	maple syrup
1 shot	espresso or ¼ cup strong coffee
·	additional milk and/or sweetener, optional, for serving

1. The night before you plan to eat the oats, place oats into a heatproof container. Place milk into a small pot; bring to a simmer. Pour it over the oats. Add salt, cinnamon, and maple syrup; stir to combine. Cover; place container into the refrigerator.

2. The next morning, prepare espresso. Take oatmeal out of the fridge; pour the shot of hot espresso over it. Add additional warm milk and/or sweetener, if desired.

— NOTE —

The idea of an affogato is the contrast of the bitter and sweet, hot and cold, and solid and liquid, so resist the urge to stir the oats; instead, eat immediately.

— VARIATION —

You can also try this recipe using hot oatmeal (I prefer steel cut oats). Prepare the oatmeal as desired; top with coffee, as above.

Green, Eggs & LATKE

PAREVE ▪ YIELDS 15 LATKES

Chanukah is very special to me because I was born on the fifth night, and I was married on my birthday. When I think of the ultimate birthday breakfast — this is it for me. Many people would expect the perfect waffle sundae, served bedside with extra sprinkles, but me? I'm all about the savory. There is nothing better to me than a crispy fried latke, some sautéed greens, and a perfectly cooked poached egg. With sriracha, of course.

PERFECT POTATO LATKES

4 large	russet (Idaho) potatoes
1 small	white onion, grated
2 large	eggs, lightly beaten
2 Tbsp	matzah meal
2 tsp	kosher salt
▪	pepper, to taste
▪	canola oil, for frying

GREENS

6 oz.	baby spinach
1 Tbsp	olive oil
▪	salt, to taste
▪	pepper, to taste

EGGS

▪	dash vinegar, for poaching
▪	eggs, for poaching
▪	sriracha, optional, for serving

TIP

Use ¼-cup measuring cup to portion out the latkes. This ensures that the latkes are the same size. When you scoop the batter into the pan, use the flat underside of the measuring cup to press down on the latke and spread it out. This creates super crispy edges.

1. **Prepare the latkes:** Peel potatoes; grate by hand or with a food processor; immediately place into a bowl of water to prevent browning. Grate the onion and set aside. Drain potatoes and put them, along with grated onion, into a clean dishtowel. Wrap tightly; squeeze out as much liquid as possible into a bowl. Let the liquid sit for a bit so the potato starch settles to the bottom. Slowly pour the liquid out of the bowl (into the sink), leaving the potato starch in the bowl.

2. Add eggs, matzah meal, salt, and pepper to the starch; stir to combine. Mix in the grated potatoes and onions. Heat oil in a skillet; add scoops of potato mixture. Fry until golden brown; flip to brown second side. Drain on paper towels.

3. **Prepare the greens:** Heat olive oil in a skillet; add spinach. Sauté until wilted; season to taste with salt and pepper.

4. **Poach the eggs:** Fill a wide saucepan ⅔-full with water; bring to a boil. Lower heat to a bare simmer; there should be small bubbles but not a rolling boil. Add a splash of vinegar to the water.

5. Crack each egg into its own small cup. Swirl the water with a spoon, creating a whirlpool; gently ease eggs into the water, working one at a time. Do not overcrowd the pan; work in batches if necessary. Cook eggs for approximately 4 minutes. Remove eggs with a slotted spoon; drain on a paper towel.

6. To serve, top the latkes with spinach, a poached egg, and sriracha, if desired.

APPETIZERS

Chicken Marsala Hamentashen

Chicken Liver Hummus

Sushichos (Sushi Nachos)

Harissa Chicken Sliders

Lachmagine Flatbreads

Kofta Stuffed Dates

Hasselback Potato Salad Bites

Plantain Chips with Tropical Guacamole

Tamarind Chicken Wings

Chilled Spring Pea Shooters

Chicken Marsala
HAMENTASHEN

MEAT • YIELDS 24 HAMENTASHEN • FREEZER FRIENDLY

Purim marks the Jews' miraculous victory over the evil Haman, whose 3-cornered hat is represented by the hamantash. I loved turning my hamantashen into a savory appetizer instead of a dessert. This perfect holiday starter is so delicious, you'll make it all year long!

2 packages	(4 sheets) puff pastry, thawed in the refrigerator overnight
1	egg, lightly beaten
1 Tbsp	olive oil
1 lb.	dark meat chicken cutlets, very finely diced
•	salt, to taste
•	pepper, to taste
1	shallot, thinly sliced
2 cloves	garlic, minced
10 oz.	baby bella mushrooms, finely chopped
½ cup	Marsala wine
2 Tbsp	flour
1 cup	chicken stock
•	fresh chopped parsley, for garnish

SPECIAL EQUIPMENT

- set of graduated triangular cookie cutters

— NOTE —

Use leftover filling and pastry scraps to make mini pot pies.

— DINNER OPTION —

Prepare Chicken Marsala Pot Pie: Add mixture to a baking dish; cover with puff pastry. Cut slits in the pastry to allow steam to escape. Bake at 375°F until pastry is puffed and golden. Or serve mixture over mashed potatoes or rice.

— VARIATIONS —

Make traditional vol au vents with prepared pastry shells or cups from the supermarket freezer section. You may also make this recipe with sweetbreads instead of chicken.

1. Preheat oven to 400°F. Line a baking sheet with parchment paper.

2. **Prepare the hamentashen:** Place thawed puff pastry on your work surface; do not roll out. Use the largest cookie cutter to cut each sheet of puff pastry into 12 large triangles (48 in total). Using the smallest cookie cutter, cut out and remove a small triangle from the center of 24 triangles. Brush the uncut triangles with beaten egg; place on prepared baking sheet. Top each triangle with the cut triangles. Using a fork, prick the dough in the center of the uncut lower triangle. Brush with beaten egg. Bake for 15-20 minutes, until puffed and golden. If the center of the dough has puffed up, press it down with your finger.

3. **Prepare the filling:** Heat oil in a frying pan over high heat. Sauté chicken until cooked through, 8-10 minutes, seasoning with salt and pepper. Remove from pan; set aside.

4. Add shallot and garlic to the pan; sauté until fragrant. Add mushrooms; cook over high heat until all the liquid evaporates and the mushrooms caramelize (if the mushrooms start to stick to the pan, add a bit more oil).

5. Add wine; cook until reduced by half. Return reserved chicken to the pan; sprinkle with flour, stirring until the flour is incorporated. Stir over medium heat until the mixture takes on some color. Add stock, salt, and pepper; cook until thickened.

6. Fill the hamentashen generously with the filling. Garnish with chopped parsley. Serve warm.

Chicken Liver
HUMMUS

MEAT • YIELDS 4 CUPS HUMMUS (12 SERVINGS)

The only thing better than a bowl of hummus with fresh, hot pita is one loaded with toppings. Hummus bassar, hummus topped with spiced ground beef or lamb, is a popular appetizer in Israel. Instead of going the traditional route, I decided to top it off with a classic Ashkenazi appetizer that I grew up on — sautéed chicken livers.

HUMMUS

1 cup	dried chickpeas
2 tsp	baking soda, divided
1 cup	good-quality tahini paste
2 cloves	garlic
¼ cup + 1 Tbsp	fresh-squeezed lemon juice
2 tsp	kosher salt
½ tsp	cumin
½ cup	ice water

LIVER

3 Tbsp	olive oil, divided
2 large	onions, sliced into half-moons
2 cloves	garlic, minced
¾ lb.	broiled chicken liver, roughly chopped
2 tsp	sweet paprika
1 tsp	smoked paprika
•	salt, to taste
•	pepper, to taste

FOR SERVING

- paprika
- fresh parsley
- sliced hardboiled eggs

1. **Prepare the hummus:** Add chickpeas and 1 teaspoon baking soda to a large bowl; cover with a few inches of water. Soak overnight.

2. Drain chickpeas and rinse. Add chickpeas and remaining teaspoon of baking soda to a pot; cover with a few inches of water. Bring to a boil; skim off any scum that rises to the surface. Reduce heat to a simmer; cook, covered, for 1 hour, until soft and tender. Drain well.

3. Stir tahini paste thoroughly before measuring, as oil and solids tend to separate. Add garlic, lemon juice, salt, cumin, and tahini paste to the bowl of a food processor fitted with the "S" blade. Puree the mixture; while the machine is running, pour ice water through the feed tube. Blend until mixture is very smooth.

4. Add drained chickpeas; blend until creamy. Adjust seasoning, adding more salt, cumin, or lemon juice, if desired.

5. **Prepare the liver:** In a large skillet, heat 2 tablespoons olive oil. Add onions; sauté until deeply golden and caramelized, about 30 minutes. Add garlic, sauté until fragrant. Add livers, remaining tablespoon oil, paprikas, salt, and pepper. Cook until the livers are heated through.

6. To plate, spread hummus onto a large shallow bowl or platter or divide between 2 bowls; top with liver. Garnish with parsley and paprika. Serve with sliced eggs.

NOTE

Kosher chicken livers are broiled to remove the blood. If purchasing fresh livers, broil before using in this recipe.

Sushichos
(SUSHI NACHOS)

PAREVE · YIELDS 8 SERVINGS

What is it about Jews and sushi? When pizza stores and supermarkets started opening satellite sushi stands a few years back, I thought it was just a passing phase, but it's become pretty clear that the trend is here to stay. Sushi salad was one of my first recipes to go viral just a few months into starting my blog and these sushi nachos are my Millennial take on that old-time favorite recipe.

8 oz. (½ pkg.)	wonton wrappers, cut in half diagonally
·	canola oil, for frying
1 lb.	sushi grade ahi tuna, cut into 3-4-inch cubes
2 Tbsp	soy sauce
2 tsp	rice vinegar
1 tsp	toasted sesame oil
½ tsp	sriracha
1	avocado, diced
4	radishes, thinly sliced
3	scallions, thinly sliced
1 sheet	nori, cut into strips
1 cup	frozen shelled edamame, thawed
½ cup	sweet sauce or teriyaki sauce
½ cup	spicy mayo (recipe follows)

1. **Prepare the chips:** Fill a shallow pan with about 1 inch of oil and bring it to medium heat. Fry the wonton wrappers until lightly browned, about 1 minute per side; they will darken as they cool. Drain on paper towels.

2. **Prepare the fish:** Combine tuna, soy sauce, rice vinegar, sesame oil, and sriracha in a small bowl. Stir to combine.

3. **Assemble the nachos:** Spread half the chips onto a platter; top with half the fish, avocado, radishes, scallions, nori, and edamame. Drizzle with sweet sauce and spicy mayo. Repeat to form a second layer. Serve immediately.

SPICY MAYO

PAREVE · YIELDS ¾ CUP

½ cup	mayonnaise
2 Tbsp	rice vinegar
2 tsp	sriracha, or to taste

· Mix well until incorporated.

NOTE

Turn this into a weeknight "poke bowl" dinner by serving the components over quinoa or brown rice instead of wonton chips.

TIP

Place the sweet sauce and spicy mayo into ziplock bags; snip off a corner of each bag. Drizzle evenly over the nachos.

Harissa
CHICKEN SLIDERS

MEAT • YIELDS 12 SERVINGS • FREEZER FRIENDLY

One of the best parts of my job as a food writer and blogger is traveling the world to give cooking demos to a range of audiences. When Federation JCA of Montreal invited me to be a part of their Jewish Food Project series, I knew I wanted to come up with a Moroccan-inspired recipe to honor the heritage of many of the attendees. Harissa — a spicy North African chili paste — and preserved lemons — a pickled condiment — are a classic Moroccan pairing, making these sliders a huge hit with my audience.

2 Tbsp	olive oil
1 small	onion, finely diced
2 cloves	garlic, minced
1 tsp	paprika
3 Tbsp	tomato paste
3	skinless, boneless chicken breasts
•	salt, to taste
•	pepper, to taste
½ cup	chicken stock
2 tsp	spicy harissa
•	juice of ½ lemon
•	Hummus (page 66), for serving
•	slider buns, for serving

1. Heat a sauté pan over medium heat; add oil. Add onions and garlic; sauté until translucent. Add paprika; continue to sauté until fragrant. Add tomato paste; stir until paste starts to deepen in color, about 2 minutes.

2. Add chicken; season, to taste, with salt and pepper. Add stock; cover the pot and bring the mixture to a gentle boil. Reduce heat; simmer for 20 minutes.

3. Remove chicken from the pot; pull it apart with two forks.

4. Add harissa and lemon juice to the sauce. Add pulled chicken to the sauce.

5. **Assemble the sliders:** Spread hummus over the slider buns; add a small mound of shredded chicken. Top with carrot slaw (below) before serving.

VARIATION

These can also be made into tacos, wraps, or grain bowls with your grain of choice.

FREEZING INSTRUCTIONS

Shredded chicken may be frozen. Thaw and reheat before serving.

PRESERVED LEMON CARROT SLAW

1 clove	garlic, minced
¼ cup	light olive oil
3 Tbsp	minced preserved lemon peel (page 20) OR juice and zest of 1 lemon
•	salt, to taste
•	pepper, to taste
3 medium	carrots, peeled and shredded
¼ cup	packed parsley OR cilantro, chopped

1. Add garlic, olive oil, lemon peel, salt, and pepper to a bowl; stir to combine.

2. Pour mixture over grated carrots; stir in the parsley.

Lachmagine
FLATBREADS

MEAT ▪ YIELDS 8 SERVINGS

One of the perks of having a Syrian mother-in-law is all of the amazing family recipes that she cooks and shares with love. My mother-in-law's lachmagine is not classic, but it's one of the best I've ever had. Instead of using prune butter or tamarind in her meat pies, she cooks down her ground beef with dried apricots for a version that's sweet but slightly tangy. Flatbreads are all the rage right now, so I simplified her recipe and turned it into a party-friendly dish that's even more appetizing when topped with a runny egg.

¾ lb.	ground beef
¼ cup	finely diced onion
½ cup	apricot jam
2 tsp	freshly squeezed lemon juice
1 (6-oz.) can	tomato paste
¼ tsp	allspice
▪	salt, to taste
1 lb.	pizza dough
2	eggs
¼ cup	toasted pine nuts, for garnish, optional

1. Preheat oven to 400°F. Line a baking sheet with parchment paper.

2. In a medium bowl, combine ground beef, onion, apricot jam, lemon juice, tomato paste, allspice, and salt.

3. Divide the pizza dough in half; roll each half into a rectangle about 11 x 7-inches, about ¼-inch thick. Place the rectangles side by side on prepared baking sheet; spread half the meat mixture over each.

4. Bake on the bottom rack of the oven for 20 minutes; remove from the oven. Break an egg into a bowl; slide onto the center of a flatbread. Repeat with remaining egg and flatbread. Return to the oven for 6 minutes, or until the egg is set. Garnish with pine nuts, if desired. Serve immediately.

Kofta Stuffed DATES

MEAT ▪ YIELDS 24 DATES

Kosherizing popular foods is one of my passions and I was determined to do so with the classic appetizer, bacon-wrapped dates. Stuffing the sweet dates with the spiced kofta filling and wrapping them in smoky kosher beef fry creates the perfect party bite that pairs well with beer. Your hubby will thank you.

1 lb.	ground chuck
2 Tbsp	grated shallot
2 cloves	garlic, minced
2 Tbsp	chopped parsley
½ tsp	cumin
½ tsp	allspice
¼ tsp	cinnamon
1 tsp	kosher salt
⅛ tsp	pepper
2 Tbsp	pine nuts
24	Medjool dates
12 slices	beef fry, sliced in half lengthwise

1. Preheat oven to 400°F.

2. In a large bowl, combine meat, shallot, garlic, parsley, spices, and pine nuts. Form the mixture into torpedo-shaped logs, each about 1 heaping tablespoon.

3. Slice open dates lengthwise, making sure not to cut all the way through. Discard pits.

4. Stuff dates with meat mixture. Wrap each date with a strip of beef fry; place on a rack set over a baking sheet. Bake for 20 minutes. Serve warm.

Hasselback Potato Salad
BITES

PAREVE • YIELDS 6-8 SERVINGS

Potato salad is one of my comfort foods, but I don't make it too often because, well, it doesn't love me as much as I love it, and also because it's just. not. pretty. I was determined to rectify that on all fronts, so I came up with an appetizing bite-size version that you can eat with your hands AND keep track of your serving size. They don't call me the hasselback queen for nothing!

2 lbs. baby red potatoes (about 20 potatoes)
½ cup mayonnaise
¼ cup sweet relish
2 tsp spicy brown mustard
• salt, to taste
• pepper, to taste
3 hard-boiled eggs
• smoked paprika, for garnish
• chives, for garnish

— NOTE —

For easier preparation, cut cooked potatoes in half; top with dressing, grated eggs, and garnish.

— VARIATION —

To make this into a classic potato salad, dice the potatoes and mix with the dressing. Place the potato salad into a serving dish and grate the eggs over it. Garnish as above.

1. Place the potatoes into a large saucepan; cover with salted water. Bring to a boil; simmer until potatoes are fork tender.

2. Carefully drain the potatoes and set aside to cool.

3. **Prepare the dressing.** Place mayonnaise, sweet relish, and mustard into a small bowl; stir to combine. Season, to taste, with salt and pepper. Add a bit of water (about 2 tablespoons) to thin the dressing.

4. To hasselback the potatoes, place each potato between two skewers and slice into thin slices resembling an accordion. The skewers will prevent you from cutting all the way through.

5. Arrange the potatoes on a serving platter; top each potato with some dressing. Using a handheld grater, grate the eggs over the potatoes; garnish with paprika and chives.

Plantain Chips
WITH TROPICAL GUACAMOLE

PAREVE ▪ YIELDS 6-8 SERVINGS

As a health-conscious foodie, I've done my fair share of diets over the years, and when the Paleo diet became a popular trend in recent years, I took the plunge. I'm much more of a savory eater, so the fact that I had to forgo sweet noshing wasn't so hard for me, but chips are another story. Plantains became my lifesaver, and I made them into everything from chips to tostones and homemade wraps. I loved these chips so much that they became a staple, even when the diet fizzled out.

2   green plantains, peeled and thinly sliced on a mandoline

▪   coconut or olive oil cooking spray

½ tsp   chili powder

▪   salt, to taste

TROPICAL GUACAMOLE

2   avocados, divided

1 clove   garlic, minced

1 small or ½ large   jalapeño, seeds and ribs removed, minced

½ small   red onion, diced small

⅓ cup   finely diced mango, peach, or papaya

¼ cup   pomegranate seeds

▪   juice of ½ lime

1 Tbsp   olive oil

▪   salt, to taste

▪   chopped cilantro, optional

1. Preheat oven to 400°F. Coat 2 baking sheets with oil spray.

2. Spread sliced plantains on prepared baking sheets. Coat generously with oil spray; sprinkle with chili powder and salt. Bake until browned and crisp, 10-15 minutes (for thin chips).

3. Cool completely before serving, as chips will crisp up as they cool.

4. **Prepare the tropical guacamole:** Peel and dice 1 avocado. Add to a bowl; mash avocado. Peel and dice the remaining avocado; add it to the bowl without mashing.

5. Add remaining ingredients; mix gently to combine. Serve with plantain chips.

— NOTE —

For thicker chips, bake for 15-20 minutes or until browned and crisp, or fry, if desired.

Tamarind
CHICKEN WINGS

MEAT ▪ YIELDS 6-8 SERVINGS ▪ FREEZER FRIENDLY

Tamarind is one of those ingredients that marrying into a Syrian family gifted me with and I've never turned back. I love adding the sweet and tangy paste, extracted from the tamarind fruit, to meatballs and roasts, and I even serve it alongside schnitzel as a dipping sauce. Tamarind has a bit of a molasses flavor, so pairing it with orange, honey, and brown sugar works wonders as a glaze for sticky chicken wings. Thank you, Danielle Renov @peaslovencarrots, for teaching me this method for perfectly crispy oven-baked wings!

2½ lbs.	chicken wings (about 20)
▪	pepper, to taste
⅓ cup	tamarind paste (see Note)
½ cup	honey
2 Tbsp	brown sugar
3 Tbsp	orange juice
¼ tsp	orange zest
1 Tbsp	chili garlic paste OR 2 tsp sriracha
1 Tbsp	sesame seeds, for garnish
▪	sliced scallions, for garnish

--- NOTE ---

I used pure tamarind paste for this recipe. If using a prepared paste with added sugar, adjust sweetness to your liking.

1. Preheat oven to 350°F. Lightly coat a baking sheet (nondisposable!) with nonstick cooking spray.

2. Rinse chicken wings; dry thoroughly with paper towels. Spread wings onto prepared baking sheet, taking care not to crowd them. Season wings with freshly ground pepper. Bake on the bottom rack of the oven until golden and crisp, 75-90 minutes.

3. In a small bowl, combine tamarind paste, honey, brown sugar, orange juice, orange zest, and chili garlic paste.

4. Transfer wings to a large bowl. Pour tamarind sauce over the wings; gently toss to coat. Transfer wings to a serving platter; garnish with sesame seeds and scallions.

Chilled Spring
PEA SHOOTERS

DAIRY OR PAREVE ▪ 16 (2-OUNCE) SERVINGS ▪ FREEZER FRIENDLY

This chilled soup shooter is a recipe that I developed for a Shavuos cooking class. When I plan a menu, I like to balance the dishes so that they all complement each other and work together. Because Shavuos is so focused on heavy cheese dishes, I like to serve appetizers that are light and refreshing, to leave room for the filling lasagna and heavy cheesecake. All those delicious, cheesy carbs are the reason I never put French onion soup on the menu and opt for a seasonal appetizer instead.

1 Tbsp	olive oil
1 large or 2 small	shallots, thinly sliced
2 cloves	garlic, minced
1 lb.	frozen peas
2 cups	vegetable stock
▪	salt, to taste
▪	pepper, to taste
8	basil leaves, plus more for garnish
½ cup	grated Parmesan cheese OR ground nuts, for garnish (see Note)
1	egg white, for garnish
▪	Fire-Roasted Grape Tomatoes (page 28), for garnish

1. Heat oil in a small stockpot over medium heat. Add shallots and garlic; sauté until translucent but not browned. Add peas, stock, salt, and pepper; bring to a boil. Reduce heat; simmer for about 5 minutes, until the peas have softened.

2. Remove from heat. Add basil; puree with an immersion blender or in a blender or food processor. Adjust seasoning, if necessary. Cool; refrigerate until chilled.

3. **Garnish the shooter cups:** Place egg white and Parmesan cheese into two shallow bowls. Dip the rim of your serving cups into egg white and then into cheese. Set aside to harden.

4. Layer a few basil leaves into a stack; roll them up. Thinly slice the basil into ribbons.

5. Pour soup into prepared serving cups. Garnish with fire-roasted tomatoes and fresh basil.

— NOTE —

To keep these pareve, omit the garnish or substitute ground blanched almonds or ground macadamia nuts for the Parmesan cheese.

SALADS & SPREADS

Beet Noodle Salad

Summer Berry & Feta Salad with Basil Lime Dressing

Kale Caesar Salad

Spinach Portobello Salad

Marinated Cauliflower Salad

Deli Pasta Salad

Pineapple Jalapeño Slaw

Busy in Brooklyn House Salad

Figgy Farro Salad

Must-Have Dips

Hawaj Garlic Confit

Beet Noodle SALAD

PAREVE · YIELDS 8 SERVINGS

I'm a huge fan of the spiralizer, and I recommend it to anyone who likes to get creative in the kitchen. You can do so much with it besides making the popular zoodles. I often share creative ideas at my cooking demos. This one always gets oohs and aahs from my audience.

3 medium	beets, greens attached
½ cup	roasted, salted pistachios
1 cup	pomegranate seeds

POMEGRANATE MOLASSES DRESSING

3 Tbsp	pomegranate molasses
2 Tbsp	red wine vinegar
2 tsp	Dijon mustard
1 Tbsp	honey, or to taste
¼ tsp	kosher salt, or to taste
⅛ tsp	pepper, or to taste
½ cup	grapeseed oil or light olive oil

NOTE

If you can't find beets with greens attached, you may use fresh arugula in place of the beet greens.

VARIATION

If you don't have a spiralizer, you can serve this salad using roasted beets using the method on page 236. Mix spring greens with diced roasted beets, pomegranate seeds, thinly sliced red onion, and pistachios. Toss with dressing before serving.

1. **Prepare the dressing:** Add dressing ingredients except oil to a bowl; stir to combine. Slowly drizzle in the oil while you whisk the dressing, until all the oil is incorporated.

2. **Prepare the salad:** Remove the greens from the beets; set greens aside. Wash the beets well (you do not need to peel them); pat dry. Using the 3mm noodle blade on a spiralizer, create beet noodles. Trim the noodles so they are bite size.

3. Place the spiralized beets into a ziplock bag. Add the dressing; toss to coat. Marinate for a few hours or up to overnight in the refrigerator.

4. Wash beet greens well; pat dry and slice thinly. Remove the noodles from the dressing; spread them onto a platter. Top with beet greens, pomegranate seeds, and pistachios. Drizzle with a few spoons of dressing from the bag.

Summer Berry & Feta Salad
WITH BASIL LIME DRESSING

DAIRY ▪ YIELDS 4 SERVINGS

This is your new must-have summer salad. Forget saving it for Shavuos or dairy Shabbos meals. You're going to want to make salad for lunch just so you can eat this. Trust me.

5 oz.	frisée or arugula
1 cup	sliced strawberries
½ cup	blueberries
⅓ cup	candied pecans
½ small	red onion, thinly sliced
1 cup	crumbled feta cheese

BASIL LIME DRESSING

⅓ cup	light olive oil
3 Tbsp	lime juice
2 Tbsp	honey
½ cup	packed fresh basil leaves
▪	salt, to taste
▪	pepper, to taste

1. **Prepare the dressing:** Place oil, lime juice, honey, basil, salt, and pepper into a blender or food processor; blend until smooth and creamy.

2. Spread the frisée on a platter; top with strawberries, blueberries, pecans, red onion, and feta. Drizzle with dressing before serving.

Kale
CAESAR SALAD

DAIRY ▪ YIELDS 6 SERVINGS

Kale Caesar is a favorite of Millennials everywhere, so it's really nothing new. What IS new is the unique blend of umami ingredients that make up the lip-smacking dressing in this recipe. I wasn't always a fan of kale; I found it bitter and hard to chew, until, that is, I learned how to prepare it. Kale needs to be tenderized for optimum enjoyment; that can be done in two ways. You can slice the kale very thinly, or put on gloves and massage the dressing into the kale leaves. I opt for the latter, and it's kale, all day every day!

10 cups	packed kale (about 10 oz.)
⅓ cup	Parmesan cheese
2 cups	Smoked Paprika Croutons (page 24)

DRESSING

¾ cup	mayonnaise
3 cloves	garlic, crushed
1½ tsp	anchovy paste
3 Tbsp	unseasoned rice vinegar
1 tsp	sriracha, or to taste
1 Tbsp	water

1. **Prepare the dressing:** In a small bowl, combine mayonnaise, garlic, anchovy paste, rice vinegar, and sriracha. Add 1 tablespoon water; stir until incorporated.

2. Place the kale into a large mixing bowl; using gloved hands, massage the dressing into the kale. Top with Parmesan and smoked paprika croutons.

NOTE

Don't be put off by the anchovies; they don't taste fishy at all, and they add an amazing depth of flavor! To make your own anchovy paste, drain a can of anchovies and puree them until a paste forms. Freeze remaining paste until ready to use.

TIP

For best results, make sure to dry the kale well after washing, or the water will dilute the dressing.

Spinach Portobello SALAD

PAREVE ▪ YIELDS 8-10 SERVINGS

When I started dreaming about writing a cookbook, about 8 years ago, this was the very first recipe that I put into my cookbook binder. It's still a crowd pleaser, and I managed to keep the recipe under wraps all these years.

2 large or 3 medium	portobello mushroom caps
1 Tbsp	olive oil
▪	salt, to taste
▪	pepper, to taste
1 (5-oz.) bag	baby spinach
1 (5-oz.) bag	mixed greens
8 oz.	heirloom grape tomatoes, cut in half
1	avocado, peeled and sliced
1 small	red onion, peeled and thinly sliced
⅓ cup	roasted, salted cashews

DRESSING

3 Tbsp	ketchup
1 clove	garlic
¼ cup	white wine vinegar
½ cup	olive oil
2 Tbsp	honey
½ tsp	paprika
½ tsp	kosher salt
¼ tsp	pepper
½ tsp	dried basil

1. Preheat oven to 400°F.

2. Place mushrooms onto a baking sheet; drizzle with olive oil. Sprinkle salt and pepper over the mushrooms; bake for 20 minutes. Cool; slice into strips. Set aside until ready to serve.

3. **Prepare the dressing:** Place all dressing ingredients into a bowl. Whisk until creamy and emulsified.

4. Place salad ingredients into a large bowl or arrange on a platter. Add dressing before serving.

Marinated Cauliflower
SALAD

PAREVE · YIELD 8-10 SERVINGS

I'm a big fan of cruciferous vegetables, cauliflower being my favorite. I love it raw, I love it roasted, and I especially love it marinated. Marinating the cauliflower gives it a lightly pickled flavor that is bright and refreshing. The za'atar adds an herbaceous punch that works really well in this recipe.

1 large	head cauliflower, separated into florets; cut into bite-size pieces
½ cup	sundried tomatoes in oil, thinly sliced
1	red onion, thinly sliced into half circles
½ cup	sliced black olives
¼ cup	capers
⅓ cup	chopped parsley
⅓ cup	olive oil
⅓ cup	apple cider vinegar
2 Tbsp	za'atar
1 Tbsp	sugar
▪	salt, to taste
▪	pepper, to taste

1. Mix all the ingredients in a bowl.

2. Marinate for one hour before serving.

Deli
PASTA SALAD

MEAT · YIELDS 12 SERVINGS

I love when dinner hosts make the effort to prepare a few special dishes for the kids. It makes the meal so much more enjoyable, especially when you have picky eaters. I try to keep that in mind whenever I have guests for Shabbos meals, and this kid-friendly pasta salad fits the bill. Don't be surprised if the adults enjoy it too!

12 oz.	farfalle pasta, prepared according to package directions
1 (11-oz.) can	corn niblets, drained
1 cup	halved grape tomatoes
2	sour pickles, diced small
1 cup (about 5 oz.)	smoked turkey, cut into strips
1 cup (about 5 oz.)	pastrami, cut into strips

DRESSING

1 cup	mayonnaise
¼ cup	Dijon mustard
¼ cup	whole grain mustard
½ cup	honey
·	salt, to taste

1. **Prepare the dressing:** In a small bowl, combine mayonnaise, mustards, and honey. Add salt, to taste.

2. In a large bowl, toss together pasta, corn, tomatoes, pickles, turkey, and pastrami.

3. Pour the dressing over the salad; stir to combine.

VARIATION

You can also use grilled chicken instead of deli meat.

Pineapple Jalapeño
SLAW

PAREVE • YIELDS 10 SERVINGS

I love a good slaw recipe, especially for family barbecues, but there's something about leaving the classic mayo-laden recipe out in the summer sun that just isn't a good idea. I came up with this fresher and lighter fruity version that goes well with grilled chicken, Asian turkey burgers, or a perfectly cooked steak.

10 oz.	shredded green cabbage
10 oz.	shredded red cabbage
3	scallions, sliced
1	jalapeño pepper, thinly sliced (remove veins and seeds to make it less spicy)
1½ cups	finely diced pineapple
⅓ cup	salted sunflower seeds, optional
2 tsp	toasted black and white sesame seeds

DRESSING

3 Tbsp	light olive oil or grapeseed oil
¼ cup	lime juice
3 Tbsp	apple cider vinegar
¼ cup	honey
½ tsp	lime zest
½ tsp	sriracha
•	salt, to taste
•	pepper, to taste

1. **Prepare the dressing:** In a small bowl, combine oil, lime juice, vinegar, honey, lime zest, sriracha, salt, and pepper.

2. Place cabbages, scallions, jalapeño, pineapple, and sunflower seeds into a large bowl. Toss together; before serving, pour on the dressing. Stir to coat. Garnish with sesame seeds.

— NOTE —

If your pineapple is very sweet, you can add a bit more sriracha to balance out the flavors.

Busy in Brooklyn
HOUSE SALAD

PAREVE · YIELDS 6-8 SERVINGS

As a busy mom of five, I have to say that finding the time to eat a healthy lunch, even when I'm recipe testing, can be very difficult. I find that taking out the time on Sunday mornings to stock the fridge really goes a long way. This salad combination was a result of throwing a little of this and a little of that into my salad bowl one day, and I've been making it ever since. I can eat this salad again and again and I don't ever get bored of it — I just switch up the protein, choosing between sliced eggs, a scoop of tuna, and, for dairy meals, feta cheese.

½ cup	quinoa
¾ cup	water
6 cups	chopped kale
1 cup	chickpeas
2 cups	diced beets (3 small beets; see Note)
¼ cup	pumpkin seeds
⅓ cup	dried cranberries

OPTIONAL TOPPING

- sliced hardboiled egg OR a scoop of tuna

DRESSING

½ cup	olive oil
¼ cup	balsamic vinegar
2 Tbsp	Dijon mustard
2 Tbsp	honey
1 large	clove garlic, minced
1 Tbsp	fresh-squeezed lemon juice
	salt, to taste
	pepper, to taste

1. **Prepare the quinoa:** Place quinoa and ¾ cup water into a small saucepan. Bring to a boil; reduce to a simmer and cook, covered, for 10 minutes. Cool for 10 minutes; fluff with a fork.

2. **Prepare the dressing:** In a small bowl, combine dressing ingredients; whisk until thick and creamy.

3. Add salad ingredients to a large bowl. Mix dressing into the salad. Top with sliced egg or tuna, if desired.

NOTES

Use vacuum-packed prepared beets or roast your own, using the method on page 236.

Check the quinoa package to see if it should be rinsed before cooking; some brands are prewashed.

Figgy FARRO SALAD

PAREVE · 8 SERVINGS

Farro, an ancient grain similar to barley, has gained traction for its health benefits and chewy texture that works well in salads, soups, and grain bowls. I love that you can dress up this dish with feta for a weekday salad, or serve it with chicken for a hearty side dish.

1½ cups	farro
6 cups	water
•	neck of butternut squash, peeled and cut into small pieces (2 cups)
1 red	onion, cut into chunks
1 Tbsp	olive oil
2 Tbsp	silan OR honey, divided
•	salt, to taste
•	pepper, to taste
⅓ cup	sliced almonds
¼ cup	light olive oil
¼ tsp	orange zest
¼ cup	fresh-squeezed orange juice
1 Tbsp	fresh-squeezed lemon juice
¼ tsp	cumin
¼ tsp	cinnamon
½ tsp	kosher salt
1 cup	diced dried figs
•	handful fresh mint, roughly chopped, optional

1. Preheat oven to 425 degrees. Line a baking sheet with parchment paper.

2. **Prepare the farro:** Place farro into a large pot with 6 cups water. Bring to a boil; reduce heat and simmer for 30 minutes. Drain. Set aside.

3. Place squash and onion onto prepared baking sheet. Toss with oil, silan, salt, and pepper. Roast until tender and caramelized, about 30 minutes, stirring occasionally.

4. Spread almonds onto a baking sheet; place into the oven toward the end of the roasting time. Toast for 3-4 minutes, until lightly browned

5. **Prepare the dressing:** In a small bowl, combine light olive oil, orange zest, orange juice, lemon juice, remaining silan, cumin, cinnamon, and salt.

6. In a large mixing bowl, combine farro, squash, red onion, figs, and dressing. Toss to combine. Season the salad with salt and pepper, to taste.

7. Add almonds just before serving. Garnish with fresh mint, if desired.

— NOTE —

Pearled farro will require less cooking time; prepare according to package directions.

Must-Have DIPS

Dips and spreads are essentials in my fridge stock. They add bursts of flavors to sandwiches and make great additions to the Shabbos table. My dips vary, depending on what I have in the pantry or which veggies are on their way out at the end of the week, but the following recipes are weekly staples. Try adding some sweet chili eggplant to your tuna sandwich (don't knock it till you try it!) and make use of your mushy tomatoes with this simple tomato jalapeño dip.

SWEET CHILI ROASTED EGGPLANT

PAREVE ▪ YIELDS APPROXIMATELY 3 CUPS

1 large	eggplant, unpeeled, cubed
3 Tbsp	olive oil
▪	salt, to taste
▪	pepper, to taste
1 (6-oz.) can	tomato paste
½ cup	sweet chili sauce
4	mini Israeli pickles in brine, diced
2 tsp	fresh-squeezed lemon juice
2 Tbsp	honey
1 clove	garlic, minced
1	scallion, chopped
▪	salt, to taste

1. Preheat oven to 425°F. Line a baking sheet with parchment paper.

2. Place eggplant on prepared baking sheet; toss with oil, salt, and pepper. Bake for 25-30 minutes, stirring occasionally.

3. Place eggplant into a large bowl. Mix with tomato paste, sweet chili sauce, pickles, lemon juice, honey, garlic, and scallions. Season, to taste, with salt.

TOMATO JALAPEÑO DIP

PAREVE ▪ YIELDS APPROXIMATELY 1 CUP

2 Tbsp	olive oil
1½ lbs.	soft tomatoes, roughly chopped (about 5 plum tomatoes)
5 cloves	garlic, sliced
1 large	jalapeño, sliced into half-moons, seeds and veins removed
▪	salt, to taste
▪	pepper, to taste

1. Heat oil in a deep skillet over medium heat; add tomatoes, garlic, and jalapeño. Cover; cook over medium heat until the tomatoes are soft and liquidy, about 20 minutes, stirring once. Season with salt and pepper.

2. Uncover the pan; continue to cook until most of the liquid evaporates, stirring every few minutes so it doesn't stick to the pan, about 10 minutes.

Pictured, clockwise from top

Pickled Turnips *(page 142),*
Hummus *(page 66) with* **Tahini** *(page 26),*
Hawaj Garlic Confit *(page 106),*
Sweet Chili Eggplant *(above),*
Tomato Jalapeño Dip *(above)*

Hawaj Garlic CONFIT

PAREVE · YIELDS 3 CUPS

You might recognize the word confit from the popular dish, "duck confit," which is duck leg slowly cooked in duck fat. The terms confit actually refers to cooking any dish slowly in fat, and olive oil is often used. Slowly cooking the garlic in olive oil completely transforms its sharp flavor into sweet buttery bites that are delicious when spread over challah. I've experimented with lots of different spices in my garlic confit, but the Yemenite spice blend hawaj wins hands-down.

2 cups	garlic cloves
1 Tbsp	hawaj for soup (see Note)
1½ tsp	kosher salt
1-1½ cups	extra virgin olive oil

1. Preheat oven to 350°F. In an oven-safe dish, combine garlic cloves, hawaj, and salt. Cover with olive oil; stir to combine.

2. Bake, uncovered, for 35 minutes, stirring once.

3. Store in the refrigerator for up to 2 weeks, or freeze for up to 2 months

NOTES

Hawaj is a Yemenite spice blend that is prepared two ways. Hawaj for coffee includes ginger, cardamom, cinnamon, and cloves; it is used in sweet applications. Hawaj for soup includes turmeric, cardamom, cumin, coriander, and cloves; it is used in savory applications.

If olive oil solidifies in the refrigerator, just place the jar into a bowl of warm water or set it on top of a warm oven to melt.

To save time, I like to buy prepeeled garlic cloves for this recipe.

VARIATION

If you can't find hawaj, you can make traditional garlic confit with fresh herbs such as rosemary or thyme and salt and pepper, or try other spices such as za'atar or shawarma spice.

USES

Add to pizza, pasta, or mashed potatoes; serve with fresh pita or challah. Use the garlic-infused oil to roast vegetables or to cook chicken or fish.

SOUPS

Curried Coconut Corn Soup

Ramen Bowls

Kale, Ale & Kielbasa Soup

Spinach Matzah Ball Minestrone Soup

Kabocha Squash Soup

Bubby's Cabbage Soup with Flanken

Smoky Split Pea soup

Cauliflower Chestnut Soup

Roasted Tomato Soup with Ravioli Croutons

Curried Coconut
CORN SOUP

PAREVE · YIELDS 8-10 SERVINGS

Corn soup is only as good as the quality of the corn so I like to make this recipe in the summer months, when I can get fresh-picked corn from the market. Like summer berries, corn is one of those ingredients best eaten in season, when it's naturally sweet and full of flavor. I love the addition of curry to balance the sweet corn.

1 Tbsp	coconut oil
3 cloves	garlic, minced
2	shallots, minced
1 heaping Tbsp	curry powder
7 ears	corn
5 cups	vegetable stock
3 Tbsp	honey
·	salt, to taste
14 oz.	canned coconut milk

1. Heat the coconut oil in a large stock pot. Add garlic and shallots; sauté until softened. Add the curry powder; sauté until fragrant.

2. Cut corn kernels from 5 ears; add corn kernels to soup. Add remaining 2 whole ears, stock, honey, and salt. Bring the mixture to a simmer; cook for 10 minutes. Remove whole ears from the soup; set aside. Cook soup for 25-30 minutes or until corn is tender. Stir in coconut milk.

3. Puree with an immersion blender. Cut kernels from reserved ears; return kernels to the soup.

— NOTE —

For silky smooth soup, use a Vitamix or strain in a fine mesh sieve before adding reserved kernels.

RAMEN BOWLS

MEAT • YIELDS 8-10 SERVINGS

Of all the food trends that have come and gone over the years, I hope the ramen bowl never dies. There's just something about a big bowl of ramen noodles that you can dress up a thousand different ways; it's pure comfort food for kids and adults alike.

2 tsp	toasted sesame oil
1	clove garlic, minced
1 tsp	freshly grated ginger
8 cups	chicken stock or bone broth (see page 34)
2 Tbsp	mirin
2 Tbsp	soy sauce
•	salt, to taste
3	skinless, boneless chicken breasts, thinly sliced
3½ oz.	shiitake mushrooms, sliced
2 cups	thinly sliced Napa cabbage or bok choy
2	carrots, julienned or peeled into ribbons
1 cup	snow peas, diagonally sliced
2 (3-oz.) pkgs	ramen, udon, or rice noodles, spice packet discarded, prepared according to package directions

OPTIONAL ADDITIONS

- zucchini noodles, spinach, bean sprouts, water chestnuts, tofu, broccoli

OPTIONAL TOPPINGS

- sriracha or gochujang, soft-boiled eggs, scallions, radishes, chili peppers, lime wedges, cilantro

—— NOTE ——

For an even more flavorful broth, soak ½ cup dried mushrooms in 2 cups boiling water and steep for 30 minutes. Strain the mixture, discard the mushrooms, and add the broth to the soup. You can also add a stalk of lemongrass to the pot in Step 1; discard after simmering the broth.

1. Heat the sesame oil in a stockpot. Add garlic and ginger; sauté until fragrant. Add stock, mirin, and soy sauce; bring soup to a simmer. Season, to taste, with salt.

2. Add chicken; simmer over low heat, stirring occasionally to keep the chicken from sticking to each other, until chicken is cooked through. Remove chicken with a slotted spoon; set aside.

3. Add mushrooms; cook until softened. Remove with a slotted spoon; set aside.

4. Before serving, add cabbage; cook for 2 minutes. Add carrots and snow peas; cook until just tender, 1-2 minutes.

5. Divide the chicken, mushrooms, and ramen between the serving bowls; add broth and vegetables. Add toppings of your choice.

—— BUILD YOUR OWN BOWL ——

To set up a BYOB bar, prepare your broth as above. Cook each vegetable separately in the broth, cooking until just tender and removing with a slotted spoon. Set out the cooked vegetables, protein (chicken, meat, or tofu), ramen, toppings, and broth and let everyone build their own bowls.

—— VARIATION ——

You may also use prepared chicken or meat. Slice thinly and add to your bowl along with the vegetables and broth.

Kale, Ale & Kielbasa SOUP

MEAT ▪ YIELDS 4-6 SERVINGS ▪ FREEZER FRIENDLY

When we were kids, my Bubby used to make the best tomato, rice, and hot dog soup that we all loved. My siblings and I would always count the slices of hot dogs in our bowls to see who got the most! Everybody loves little bites of franks in their soup, so I've created this more adult-friendly version for everyone to enjoy.

2 (15-oz.) cans	cannellini beans
1 (12-oz.) pkg	Kielbasa sausage, or 4 sausages
1 small	onion, diced small
2 stalks	celery, diced
2	parsnips, peeled and diced
3 cloves	garlic, minced
1 Tbsp	olive oil, if necessary
1 (12-oz.) bottle	ale, optional
4 cups	beef or chicken stock
2	bay leaves
▪	salt, to taste
▪	pepper, to taste
2 cups	chopped kale

1. Drain and rinse beans from 1 can; add beans to a bowl. With a potato masher, mash beans; set aside.

2. Drain and rinse the beans from the remaining can; set side.

3. Cut sausages into ¼-inch thick slices. Add sliced sausages to a soup pot; place over medium heat. Slowly cook the sausages until the fat is rendered and they start to caramelize. Remove sausage slices from the pot. You should have about 2 tablespoons rendered fat. If not enough fat has rendered, add about 1 tablespoon olive oil.

4. Add onion, celery, parsnips, and garlic to the pot; sauté in the rendered fat until softened and starting to brown.

5. Add the ale; simmer until reduced by half. If omitting ale, continue to Step 6.

6. Add whole beans, stock, bay leaves, salt, and pepper; bring to a boil. Reduce heat to a simmer. Add mashed beans; stir to incorporate. Cook for 20 minutes. Discard bay leaves.

7. Add sautéed sausages and kale to the pot; cook until kale has wilted.

Spinach Matzah Ball
MINESTRONE SOUP

PAREVE ▪ YIELDS 8-10 SERVINGS

Minestrone soup is one of my kids' most-requested dishes and it's how I get my pickiest to eat vegetables. My secret is using alphabet pasta in the soup instead of the traditional ditalini. Once I got my kids eating the veggies, I was determined to have them eat spinach, so I hid it in the matzah balls. They loved it so much that I started putting spinach in my matzah balls all the time, even in traditional chicken soup.

1 large	onion, diced
3 cloves	garlic, minced
1 large stalk	celery, diced
1 Tbsp	olive oil
3 heaping Tbsp	tomato paste
1 (28-oz.) can	diced tomatoes, with their liquid
1 tsp	dried basil
1 tsp	dried oregano
8 cups	vegetable stock
▪	salt, to taste
▪	pepper, to taste
2	eggs
1 Tbsp	canola oil
1 packet	matzah ball mix
¼ cup	chopped spinach (squeeze thawed frozen spinach to measure ¼ cup)
2	carrots, peeled and julienned
1 large	zucchini, julienned
6 oz.	fine egg noodles OR alphabet pasta, prepared according to package directions

1. In a 6-quart stock pot, sauté onion, garlic, and celery in olive oil until translucent. Add tomato paste; sauté until aromatics are fragrant and evenly coated. Add tomatoes with their liquid, basil, oregano, stock, salt, and pepper. Stir to combine the ingredients; bring soup to a boil. Lower the heat; simmer for 15 minutes.

2. **Meanwhile, prepare the matzah balls:** Beat eggs with oil in a bowl. Add matzah ball mix and spinach; stir with a fork until evenly combined. Refrigerate for 10 minutes.

3. Add carrots and zucchini to the soup. With wet hands, form matzah ball batter into small balls; place into simmering soup. Cook for 15 minutes.

4. Add egg noodles before serving.

VARIATION

If you don't have a julienne peeler, you may dice the carrot and zucchini and add to the pot after sautéing the onion, garlic, and celery. After several minutes, add the tomato paste and continue as above. Cook the soup until the vegetables are tender before adding the matzah balls.

Kabocha Squash SOUP

PAREVE • YIELDS 6-8 SERVINGS • FREEZER FRIENDLY

Kabocha, also known as Japanese squash, is definitely one of the lesser-known pumpkins, but I grew up on it. My mom used to call it kaboochee squash, so when she sent me to the store to buy it, they never quite knew what I was talking about! Kabocha squash is quite difficult to slice, so I love the idea of roasting it whole, no peeling or cutting required. Its flesh is rich and dense, and its sweet, velvety texture is far superior to that of its more popular cousins.

1 (3-4-lb.)	kabocha squash
3-4 cups	vegetable stock
2 tsp	brown sugar
1 tsp	pure maple syrup
3 Tbsp	white miso paste
1 tsp	sriracha, plus more for garnish
1 cup	canned coconut milk, plus more for garnish
•	salt, to taste
2	scallions, thinly sliced
1 Tbsp	toasted sesame seeds
•	toasted sesame oil, for garnish

1. Preheat oven to 400°F. Place squash onto a baking sheet. Cut a few slits into it with a sharp knife. Roast the squash for 1 hour, flipping it over after 30 minutes.

2. Remove squash from the oven; set aside to cool. Once cooled, slice the squash in half and remove the seeds. Scoop out all the flesh; place it into a 6-quart pot.

3. Add stock, brown sugar, maple syrup, miso paste, and sriracha to the pot; bring the mixture to a simmer.

4. Cook for 10 minutes; puree with an immersion blender. Stir in coconut milk. Adjust consistency by adding more stock or coconut milk, if desired. Add salt to taste.

5. Ladle the soup into serving bowls; drizzle with coconut milk and sriracha. Garnish with scallions and sesame seeds. Add a drizzle of toasted sesame oil, if desired.

Bubby's Cabbage Soup
WITH FLANKEN

MEAT ▪ YIELDS APPROXIMATELY 8 QUARTS ▪ FREEZER FRIENDLY

*My dear Bubby Hecht was a wonderful cook who put love and soul into all of her dishes.
She took tremendous pride in my accomplishments, and after years of us talking about my
writing a book, she was so happy to hear that my dreams were finally becoming reality.
I wish Bubby could be here to see her delicious cabbage soup in print, but I know she is
shepping nachas from on high.*

1 medium head	green cabbage, sliced
1	onion, sliced
2	green apples, peeled and diced or grated
2	very ripe tomatoes, diced
½ cup	golden raisins
2 lbs.	boneless flanken
1 lb.	marrow bones
3 (15-oz.) cans	tomato sauce
⅓ cup	sugar, or to taste
▪	salt, to taste
▪	pepper, to taste
▪	juice of ½ lemon

1. Place all ingredients into a 10-quart stockpot. Using an empty tomato sauce can to measure, add 7 cans (about 3 quarts) of water. Bring the mixture to a boil.

2. Lower the heat; simmer for 3 hours, until the broth has thickened and the meat is soft and tender.

3. Remove meat from the pot. Use two forks to shred the meat, or cut it into chunks. Return meat to the pot; stir to distribute meat throughout the soup.

NOTE

*I've written this recipe the way my Bubby always made
it, but if you'd like to develop more flavor, at Step 1, sear
the flanken and bones in the pot, remove, and sauté the
onions in the drippings. Add the remaining ingredients to
the pot; continue as above.*

TIP

*To make this recipe more kid-friendly,
put the raisins into a cheesecloth before adding to
the pot; remove before serving.*

Smoky
SPLIT PEA SOUP

MEAT ▪ YIELDS 8 SERVINGS

This is the soup that gets us through the winter. When the snow falls and we're stranded inside without a fireplace to gather around, this is the bowl of pure comfort that warms us from the inside out. Thousands of Busy in Brooklyn fans agree.

2 Tbsp	olive oil
2	leeks, white and pale green parts only, chopped
5 cloves	garlic, minced
2 large	carrots, peeled and diced
2 stalks	celery, diced
2 cups	split peas, picked over and rinsed
3	bay leaves
5 sprigs	thyme
1	smoked turkey leg
4 cups	chicken stock
4 cups	water
▪	salt, to taste
▪	pepper, to taste

1. Heat olive oil in an 8-quart stockpot. Add leeks and garlic; sauté until fragrant. Add carrots and celery. When they begin to soften, add split peas, bay leaves, and thyme; sauté for 2 minutes.

2. Add turkey leg to the pot; add stock and water. Bring to boil, lower the heat, and simmer for 1 hour. Discard bay leaves and thyme sprigs.

3. Remove the turkey leg from the soup; shred turkey. Return shredded turkey to the soup; season with salt and pepper, to taste. Adjust the consistency by adding more water, if desired.

4. **Optional:** Serve with Thyme Dumplings (below).

NOTES

While I prefer to cook the dumplings separately, you can also cook them directly in the simmering soup just before serving.

This soup can also be cooked in a crockpot. To make this for a Shabbos day meal, add an extra cup of water.

THYME DUMPLINGS (OPTIONAL)

1 cup	flour
½ tsp	kosher salt
1½ tsp	baking powder
1 Tbsp	oil
½ cup	lukewarm water
1 Tbsp	chopped fresh thyme

1. Whisk together flour, salt, and baking powder. Add remaining ingredients, stirring well to form a soft dough.

2. Drop teaspoons of dough into a pot of boiling water; simmer until they rise to the top. Remove with a slotted spoon; add to the soup.

Cauliflower Chestnut
SOUP

PAREVE • YIELDS 6-8 SERVINGS • FREEZER FRIENDLY

I love a good creamy soup, but only if it's minus the actual cream. The chestnuts give this soup a velvety texture and lend a sweet flavor that balances really well with the cauliflower. Don't skip the twice-roasted chestnuts; they add a much-needed crunch to balance out the dish.

2 Tbsp	olive oil
1	leek, white and pale green part only, sliced
3 cloves	garlic, minced
24 oz.	frozen cauliflower
4 cups	vegetable stock
2 (3.5-oz.) bags	roasted chestnuts
3 sprigs	thyme
•	salt, to taste
•	pepper, to taste
1½ cups	water
•	Herbes de Provence Twice-Roasted Chestnuts, optional garnish (page 310)

1. Heat olive oil in a soup pot over medium heat. Add leek; sauté until tender and starting to brown. Add garlic; sauté until fragrant. Add remaining ingredients; bring to a boil. Reduce heat to a simmer; cook,, covered, until cauliflower is tender, about 10 minutes.

2. Discard thyme sprigs. Blend soup with an immersion blender. Adjust the consistency by adding additional water or stock, if desired.

3. Garnish with Herbes de Provence Twice-Roasted Chestnuts, optional.

Roasted Tomato Soup
WITH RAVIOLI CROUTONS

DAIRY · YIELDS 6 SERVINGS · FREEZER FRIENDLY

Tomato soup has never been a dish that stands on its own, but rather a means to an even better accompaniment — grilled cheese. Everybody loves a good grilled cheese sandwich dunked in tomato soup, but this fun twist beats that classic combo.

3 lbs.	ripe plum tomatoes (about 10)
2	shallots, peeled
6 cloves	garlic, peeled
¼ cup	olive oil
·	salt, to taste
·	pepper, to taste
1-2 cups	vegetable stock
½ tsp	dried oregano
·	good quality olive oil, for garnish
·	Parmesan cheese, for garnish
·	ravioli croutons (at right)
·	fresh basil, for garnish

1. Preheat the oven to 450°F. Slice tomatoes and shallots in half lengthwise; place them cut-side-down on a baking sheet along with garlic cloves. Coat vegetables with olive oil; season with salt and pepper. Roast for 35 minutes.

2. Place the roasted vegetables with their juices into a pot. Add stock (the amount depends on the juiciness of your tomatoes) and oregano; bring to a boil. Simmer for 10 minutes. Season, to taste, with salt and pepper.

3. Using an immersion blender or food processor, puree soup until smooth. Adjust the consistency by adding more stock, if needed.

4. Ladle soup into cups; garnish with olive oil, ravioli croutons, Parmesan, and fresh basil.

RAVIOLI CROUTONS

½ cup	panko crumbs
¼ cup	Parmesan cheese
¼ tsp	oregano
¼ tsp	basil
⅛ tsp	kosher salt
2	eggs, lightly beaten
·	salt, to taste
·	pepper, to taste
1 (13-oz.) pkg	frozen cheese ravioli
·	canola oil, for frying

1. In a shallow bowl, mix panko crumbs, Parmesan, oregano, basil, and salt. In a separate bowl, lightly beat eggs with salt and pepper.

2. Working in batches, dip ravioli into the eggs, shake off the excess, and then dip into the Parmesan crumbs.

3. Heat 1 inch of oil in a skillet.

4. Fry a few breaded ravioli at a time, until golden brown on both sides, about 3 minutes. Drain on paper towels.

— NOTE —

If you don't have plum tomatoes, you can use any tomatoes (or a mix!) that you have on hand. Seasonal tomatoes will yield the best results. If tomatoes are out of season and the soup tastes very acidic, add a pinch of sugar to balance out the flavors.

FISH

Pesto Zoodles with Flaked Lemon Salmon

Kani Fried Rice

Miso Glazed Salmon

Lemon Pepper Red Snapper

Gefilte Fish "Pizza"

Everything Bagel Tuna Patties

Shawarma Fish Laffos

Moroccan Fish Cakes

Pesto Zoodles
WITH FLAKED LEMON SALMON

PAREVE ▪ YIELDS 4 SERVINGS.

When the world went zoodle-crazy with the advent of the spiralizer, I hopped right on board and never looked back. I'm not embarrassed to say that I've come to like zoodles even more than pasta, and I've gotten so many followers to follow suit. While my cheesy zoodle marinara has captured the love of kids worldwide, this pesto version, with flaked lemon salmon, is lighter, healthier, and makes a complete meal.

PESTO ZOODLES

2 large	zucchinis
¾ cup	Spinach Pistachio Pesto (page 36) or store-bought pesto
▪	fresh-squeezed lemon juice, to taste
▪	salt, to taste
▪	pepper, to taste

FLAKED LEMON SALMON

4	salmon fillets
▪	salt, to taste
▪	pepper, to taste
▪	zest and juice of 1 lemon
2 Tbsp	olive oil

─── VARIATION ───

For dairy meals, omit fish; serve with feta and grape tomatoes.

1. **Prepare the zoodles:** Using a spiralizer or julienne peeler, create zucchini noodles. Stir in the pesto until zoodles are well coated; add olive oil as needed if the pesto is thick. Season with salt and pepper. Add lemon juice to taste. Set aside to marinate and soften while you prepare the salmon.

2. **Prepare the flaked salmon:** Preheat oven to 400°F. Place salmon into a baking dish; season with salt and pepper. Rub with lemon zest; drizzle with lemon juice and olive oil.

3. Bake for 15 minutes. Using a fork, flake the salmon into small pieces.

4. Divide zoodles between individual plates; top with salmon. Garnish with freshly ground pepper and lemon zest, if desired. Serve immediately.

Kani
FRIED RICE

PAREVE ▪ YIELDS 4-6 SERVINGS

Fried rice makes a regular appearance at our dinner table because I love to use up leftovers in the form of a one-pot meal. I usually go with chicken or meat, but ever since we instituted Meatless Mondays, I'm always looking for new ways to dress up old favorites without meat or poultry. My kids are fans of sushi made with kani (mock crab sticks), so I came up with this fried rice variation.

3	eggs, beaten
pinch	salt
2 tsp	toasted sesame oil
1 Tbsp	grapeseed or canola oil, plus more if needed
5	scallions, whites and greens separated, chopped
2 cloves	garlic, minced
½ cup	shredded carrot
½ cup	shelled frozen edamame, thawed
8 sticks	kani, chopped
▪	salt, to taste
2 cups	short grain brown rice, prepared according to package directions
2 Tbsp	soy sauce
1 Tbsp	honey

1. Heat a deep nonstick skillet or wok; coat with cooking spray. Add a pinch of salt to the eggs; scramble them in the pan. Remove from pan; wipe skillet with a paper towel.

2. Heat the skillet over medium heat; add sesame and grapeseed oils. Add chopped scallion whites, garlic, carrot, and edamame; sauté until vegetables have softened, about 3 minutes. Add kani; sauté until heated through. Season with salt. Add rice; sauté until incorporated.

3. Add soy sauce, honey, and kosher salt, to taste; stir until incorporated. Stir in scrambled eggs and chopped scallion greens. Serve immediately.

Miso Glazed
SALMON

PAREVE • YIELDS 8 SERVINGS

Miso is a fermented soybean paste that comes in varying degrees of fermentation. White miso has a sweet taste and is an umami-rich flavor enhancer. The combination in this dish can only be matched by the beautiful presentation!

¼ cup	white miso paste
1½ tsp	grated ginger
2 cloves	garlic, minced
1 tsp	soy sauce
1 Tbsp	rice vinegar
2 tsp	brown sugar
1 whole side	of salmon
2 large	Portobello mushrooms, thinly sliced
1 Tbsp	olive oil
▪	salt, to taste
▪	pepper, to taste
▪	toasted sesame seeds, for garnish
▪	sliced scallions, for garnish

1. Preheat oven to 400°F.

2. In a bowl, combine miso paste, ginger, garlic, soy sauce, vinegar, and brown sugar.

3. Brush the mixture over the salmon; place mushroom slices over it, slightly overlapping. Brush mushrooms with olive oil; season with salt and pepper.

4. Bake, uncovered, for 25 minutes.

5. Garnish with scallions and sesame seeds.

Lemon Pepper
RED SNAPPER

PAREVE • YIELDS 6 SERVINGS

My best recipes are the ones that occur organically. I don't really plan them, they kind of just happen. I prepared this fish on a whim, based on the ingredients I had in my fridge, and when I shared the recipe step by step in my Instagram story, I wasn't expecting so many people to follow suit. Days and weeks later, I received images of the fish that people had made based on my basic instructions, telling me it was the best fish they ever had. I hope you agree!

1 cup	parsley
2	scallions
2 cloves	garlic
▪	zest of 1 lemon
▪	juice of 1 lemon
¼ cup	olive oil, divided
▪	salt, to taste
▪	pepper, to taste
1 (2-lb.)	whole red snapper, butterflied
1	lemon, sliced
1 tsp	lemon pepper seasoning
1 bunch	tomatoes on the vine
1 bunch	scallions

1. Preheat oven to 425°F. Line a baking sheet with parchment paper.

2. Place parsley, scallions, garlic, lemon zest, lemon juice, and 2 tablespoons olive oil into the bowl of a food processor fitted with the "S" blade. Pulse until a paste forms; season with salt and pepper.

3. Open the fish; spread the paste over the flesh. Top with lemon slices; close fish. Sprinkle fish with lemon pepper seasoning. Place on prepared baking sheet.

4. Place the tomatoes and scallions alongside the fish; season with salt and pepper. Drizzle remaining olive oil over the pan.

5. Bake for 25-30 minutes.

NOTES

To serve the fish as pictured, ask your fishmonger to leave the head and tail on the fish when butterflying it.

If you don't have lemon pepper seasoning, you can use lemon zest, salt, and pepper instead.

VARIATION

You may use branizo or any other whole white-fleshed fish of your choice.

Gefilte Fish "PIZZA"

PAREVE ▪ YIELDS 8 SERVINGS ▪ FREEZER FRIENDLY

*Gefilte fish patties are a family favorite; one week, I defrosted my gefilte fish,
but I didn't have the time to fry the patties individually. I decided to spread the defrosted
loaf into a giant patty — and the gefilte fish pizza was born.*

1 (20-oz.) pkg	frozen gefilte fish, thawed
1	egg
1 Tbsp	matzah meal
3 Tbsp	canola oil
1	carrot
1 cup	arugula
1	baby Chioggia beet or watermelon radish, thinly sliced on a mandoline
¼ cup	Quick Pickled Onions (page 22)

HORSERADISH CREAM

3 Tbsp	mayonnaise
¼ cup	horseradish with beets

— NOTES —

*If the fish seems to have browned too quickly, but
the inside is not cooked enough, bake at 350°F for
10-15 minutes, or until slightly puffed.*

*If desired, lightly dress the salad with olive oil,
lemon juice, salt, and pepper.*

— VARIATION —

*You may bake the gefilte fish by spreading it into a
greased 10-inch round pan. Brush the top with oil;
bake at 350°F, uncovered, for approximately 45 minutes,
or until slightly puffed and browned.
Alternatively, before baking, brush the top with
mayonnaise and sprinkle with panko breadcrumbs for a
crispy coating.*

1. **Prepare the fish:** In a medium bowl, combine gefilte fish, egg, and matzah meal.

2. Heat oil in a 10-inch frying pan; spread fish mixture evenly in the pan. Cook over low/medium heat until golden brown, abut 8 minutes. Place a plate over the pan; flip fish onto it. Gently slide the fish back into the pan to fry the other side. Cook until golden brown, about 8 more minutes. (After cooling, fish may be frozen, if desired.)

3. **Prepare the horseradish cream:** Add mayonnaise and horseradish to a bowl; mix to combine.

4. Using a vegetable peeler, peel the carrot into ribbons.

5. Spread the horseradish cream over the fish; top with arugula, carrot ribbons, beet, and pickled onions. Cut into wedges to serve.

Everything Bagel
TUNA PATTIES

PAREVE ▪ YIELDS 12 PATTIES ▪ FREEZER FRIENDLY

My kids are not big fish eaters. Sure, they'll chow down on crunchy fish and chips, and thankfully they do like gefilte fish, but other than that, they just find fish too, well … fishy. I was determined to come up with a kid-friendly weeknight fish dish, so I took inspiration from the classic tuna bagel in the form of patties. These Everything Bagel Tuna Patties were a big hit, and they've become a regular part of our dinner rotation.

4 (6-oz.) cans	chunk white albacore tuna in water, drained and flaked
3 Tbsp	pickle relish
¼ cup	mayonnaise
¼ cup	panko breadcrumbs
2	eggs
1 Tbsp	yellow mustard
2 tsp	lemon juice
▪	salt, to taste
▪	pepper, to taste
▪	canola oil, for frying

EVERYTHING BAGEL BREADING

1 cup	panko breadcrumbs
1 Tbsp	poppy seeds
1 Tbsp	sesame seeds
2 tsp	onion flakes
2 tsp	garlic flakes
½ tsp	kosher salt

1. **Prepare the patties:** In a bowl, combine tuna, pickle relish, mayonnaise, panko breadcrumbs, eggs, mustard, lemon juice, salt, and pepper. Using a ¼-cup measuring cup, form the mixture into patties.

2. **Prepare the breading:** In a shallow bowl, combine panko breadcrumbs, poppy seeds, sesame seeds, onion flakes, garlic flakes, and salt. Press tuna patties into the crumb mixture, coating all sides.

3. Heat oil in a frying pan over medium-high heat; fry patties until golden; flip and fry second side till golden. Alternatively, bake the patties: Preheat oven to 425°F. Coat a baking sheet with cooking spray; place patties on the tray. Spray patties generously with cooking spray; bake for 20 minutes, until browned and crispy.

4. Serve with a side of fries or mashed potatoes, if desired.

── VARIATION ──

To make tuna patty melts, top each fried or baked patty with mozzarella or cheddar cheese; bake at 425°F until melted.

Shawarma
FISH LAFFOS

DAIRY OR PAREVE ▪ YIELDS 6 SERVINGS

If I had to pick a favorite spice blend, it would have to be shawarma spice. I love it on everything. It works with meat (try spicing up some ground beef crumbles and serving on hummus), chicken (my kids love shawarma-spiced drumsticks), roasted chickpeas (best snack everrrrr), roasted cauliflower, and, yes, even fish. Shawarma-spiced fish laffos (laffa + tacos) are my Millennial take on the traditional laffa, down to the pickled turnips (make them ahead of time so they'll be ready when you are). And since the fish is pareve, the tahini crema will make you see the sesame paste in a whole new light!

See photo on following page.

PICKLED TURNIPS

3 small	turnips, thinly sliced on a mandolin
1 small	beet, cut into wedges
1	bay leaf
2 cloves	garlic
½ cup	red wine vinegar
1½ cups	water
2 Tbsp	kosher salt
1 Tbsp	sugar

1. Place sliced turnips, beets, bay leaf, and garlic into a glass jar.

2. In a small saucepan, bring vinegar, water, salt, and sugar to a simmer. Pour the mixture over the vegetables; set aside to cool.

3. Refrigerate until ready to use. Depending on how thinly you slice the turnips, the pickles will be ready overnight or after 2-4 days.

SHAWARMA SPICE MIX

1 Tbsp	ground cumin
1 Tbsp	ground coriander
2 tsp	paprika
1 tsp	turmeric
½ tsp	garlic powder
½ tsp	allspice
¼ tsp	ground cinnamon
¼ tsp	pepper
½ tsp	kosher salt

- Mix all ingredients in a bowl and stir to combine.

FISH

3 large firm white fish fillets, such as tilapia, flounder, snapper, or cod (1½-lbs.)
1 batch shawarma spice mix (facing page) OR ¼ cup store-bought shawarma spice mix
¼ cup olive oil
- juice of ½ lemon
- salt, to taste

1. Preheat oven to 400°F. Coat a baking sheet with nonstick cooking spray.

2. Combine the shawarma spice mix and oil in a small bowl; brush over the fish fillets, coating generously on both sides. Place fillets on prepared baking sheet; squeeze lemon juice over fish. Season lightly with salt. Bake, uncovered, for 20 minutes.

CABBAGE SLAW

10 oz. shredded red cabbage
2 Tbsp light olive oil
- juice of ½ lemon
- salt, to taste

- Stir together cabbage, oil, lemon juice, and salt. Marinate for 10 minutes.

TAHINI CREMA

¼ cup tahini
¼ cup water
¼ cup plain Greek yogurt
2 Tbsp chopped parsley
1 clove garlic, minced
¼ tsp lemon zest
- juice of ½ lemon
- salt, to taste

- Combine all crema ingredients in a bowl, whisking until creamy. If needed, add additional water until desired consistency is reached.

─── NOTE ───

For pareve meals, omit Greek yogurt.

ASSEMBLE THE LAFFOS

FOR SERVING

6 mini laffas or pitas
- parsley
- harissa or schug, optional
- lemon wedges

1. Heat the laffas briefly over an open flame until blistered.

2. Divide the fish between the laffas; top with cabbage slaw, tahini crema, pickled turnips, harissa, and parsley.

3. Serve with lemon wedges.

─── VARIATION ───

If you don't have time to make the pickled turnips (or you don't like them), you may use pickled onions (see page 22) instead.

Moroccan
FISH CAKES

PAREVE ▪ YIELDS 8 SERVINGS ▪ FREEZER FRIENDLY

As a recipe writer, I get a real thrill out of fusing Ashkenazi and Sephardi cuisine. I love introducing Sephardim to Ashkenazi ingredients, and vice versa. Now, if you've ever met a Moroccan, you know that they won't touch gefilte fish with a ten-foot pole, and Ashkenazim like their gefilte fish traditional. This mashup, which I've made on my blog in the form of fish balls, has converted gefilte fish haters and lovers alike.

FISH CAKES

1 (20-oz.)	loaf gefilte fish, defrosted
1	egg
1½ Tbsp	matzah meal
2 Tbsp	chopped parsley OR cilantro
2 cloves	garlic, minced
1 tsp	cumin
¼ tsp	turmeric
▪	salt, to taste
▪	pepper, to taste
▪	canola oil, for frying

SAUCE

2 Tbsp	olive oil
6 cloves	garlic, sliced
1	red bell pepper, seeds and veins removed, sliced into half-moons
1	carrot, peeled and thinly sliced diagonally
1 (15-oz.) can	tomato sauce
1 cup	canned chickpeas, rinsed and drained
1 tsp	paprika
2 tsp	freshly squeezed lemon juice
2 Tbsp	honey
▪	salt, to taste
▪	pepper, to taste
▪	handful fresh parsley

1. **Prepare the fish:** In a mixing bowl, combine gefilte fish, egg, matzah meal, parsley, garlic, cumin, turmeric, salt, and pepper. Refrigerate while you prepare the sauce.

2. **Prepare the sauce:** Heat oil in deep skillet over medium high heat; sauté garlic, red pepper, and carrot until they begin to caramelize. Add tomato sauce, chickpeas, paprika, lemon juice, honey, salt, and pepper. Bring to a simmer; cook until the vegetables are soft, about 15 minutes. Add parsley.

3. Remove fish mixture from the fridge; with damp hands, form it into 8 patties. Heat oil in a frying pan over medium heat; fry patties until golden brown on each side. Drain on paper towels.

4. To serve, plate fish cakes individually and spoon the sauce over them, or heat the fish cakes in the sauce and serve on a platter.

--- NOTE ---

If the fish cakes brown before they are fully cooked on the inside, finish cooking in the oven at 350°F for about 15 minutes, until puffed and golden.

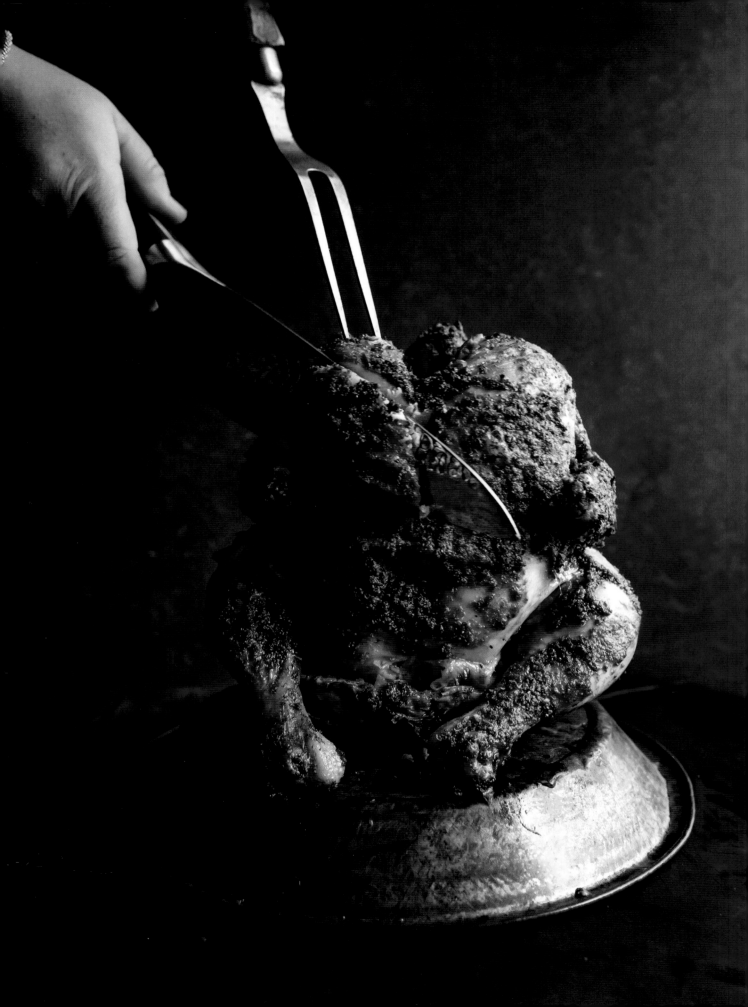

POULTRY

Pineapple Rotisserie Chicken

Corn Chex Nuggets with Maple Mustard Dip

Olive Chicken

Chicken Pesto Avocado Wraps

Ma's Stuffed Cornish Hens

Curried Shake & Bake Drumsticks

Braised Lemon Chicken with Leeks

Maple Chili Spatchcock Chicken

Honey Roasted Za'atar Chicken with Dried Fruit

Fennel & Orange Turkey Roast with Capers

Pineapple
ROTISSERIE CHICKEN

MEAT ▪ YIELDS 4-6 SERVINGS ▪ FREEZER FRIENDLY

It was Justin Chapple's "Mad Genius Tips" in Food and Wine magazine that turned me on to the now-famous Bundt pan roasted chicken recipe that's featured on my blog. Cooking the chicken upright in a Bundt pan yields a supremely crispy skin and moist, evenly cooked bird. While many of my followers were intrigued, I found that people didn't want to make their pareve Bundt pans meaty, so they lost out on this fantastic preparation. Not anymore! Now you can enjoy your pineapple and even use the core as a nifty chicken stand! Cooking the chicken this way moistens it from the inside out, so you're left with supremely moist bird. There is even the slightest hint of pineapple flavor in the flesh; if you're a smoking aficionado, I bet this method would work especially well in the smoker!

1	pineapple
1 (3-lb.)	whole chicken
¼ cup	olive oil
1 batch	House Rub (page 30)
▪	salt, to taste

— NOTES —

Using a shallow receptacle is important because a deeper pan will allow steam to build up around the chicken, and steam inhibits the skin from crisping up.

Use the leftover pineapple from this recipe to make Pineapple Jalapeño Slaw (page 98).

— VARIATION —

For easy weeknight grilled chicken, mix 2 tablespoons spice rub with 2 tablespoons olive oil. Rub the mixture over 4 skinless, boneless chicken breasts; marinate in the refrigerator for 1 hour. Grill or broil for approximately 5 minutes per side, or bake at 425°F for 25 minutes.

— TIP —

If you are using a very ripe pineapple, and you are worried that it won't hold up during cooking, press a skewer through the core of the pineapple to give it extra stability.

1. To create a rotisserie stand from the pineapple, use a large chef's knife (NOT a paring knife) to cut the crown and stem from the pineapple so that it stands flat. Slice around the circumference of the pineapple 1½ inches from the bottom, taking care not to cut through the pineapple core. Cut four vertical slices from around the pineapple, only up until the 1½-inch-thick pineapple base (see diagram).

2. Preheat oven to 400°F. Set out a cast iron skillet, shallow Dutch oven, or baking sheet. Do not use a disposable pan.

3. Rinse chicken; pat dry thoroughly. In a small bowl, combine olive oil and house rub to create a paste. Rub the paste all over the chicken. Season the chicken, to taste, with kosher salt. Place the core of the pineapple through the cavity of the chicken so that the base of the chicken rests on the pineapple stand. Place the chicken into the skillet or pan. Bake for 60-75 minutes, or until the internal temperature reaches 165°F.

4. To serve, cut the chicken into quarters and serve with pan drippings, if desired.

Corn Chex Nuggets
WITH MAPLE MUSTARD AIOLI

MEAT • YIELDS 8 SERVINGS • FREEZER FRIENDLY

Shnitzel is every kid's dream dinner, and I'm determined to keep it fun and kid-friendly! We love to play around with different breading — from flavored panko to tortilla chips and bissli — but this Corn Chex version wins the award for the ultimate crunchy nugget. My kids take turns crushing the cereal, throwing the bag against the wall and even stomping on it at times. I guess that's why it's their most-requested version of shnitzel.

1½ lbs.	skinless and boneless chicken breasts, cut into bite-size nuggets or strips
8 cups	Corn Chex cereal
½ cup	flour
•	salt, to taste
•	pepper, to taste
½ tsp	chili powder
2	eggs
3 Tbsp	pure maple syrup (NOT pancake syrup)
3 Tbsp	mustard

MAPLE MUSTARD AIOLI

½ cup	mayonnaise
2 Tbsp	maple syrup
2 Tbsp	mustard
¼ tsp	chili powder

1. Heat oven to 400°F. Coat 2 baking sheets generously with nonstick cooking spray.

2. Place cereal into a large ziplock bag; crush with your hands until crumbs form.

3. Place flour into a shallow dish; season with salt, pepper, and chili powder. In a second shallow dish, stir together eggs, maple syrup, mustard, salt, and pepper. Place crushed cereal into a third shallow dish.

4. Dip chicken nuggets into flour mixture, then into egg mixture, and then into cereal, shaking off the excess between each step. Spread chicken nuggets on prepared baking sheets in a single layer, taking care not to crowd the pans. Bake for 12-15 minutes or until the nuggets are crispy and the chicken is cooked through.

5. **Prepare the maple mustard aioli:** In a small bowl, combine mayonnaise, maple syrup, mustard, and chili powder.

6. Serve chicken with dipping sauce.

Olive CHICKEN

If you've never cooked with pargiyot (dark meat chicken cutlets), put it on your to-do list. I prefer them to chicken breasts because — unlike white meat cutlets — they don't dry out, even if you overcook them. Try them with shawarma spice for an easy weeknight dinner.

3 oz.	tomato paste (heaping 1/4 cup)
1 tsp	dried oregano
1 tsp	dried basil
6	dark meat chicken cutlets
•	salt, to taste
•	pepper, to taste
½ cup	sliced green olives with pimentos, sliced
½ cup	sliced black olives, sliced
2	ripe tomatoes, diced
1	red onion, thinly sliced into half-moons
2 Tbsp	olive oil
pinch	red pepper flakes, optional

1. Preheat oven to 400°F.

2. In a small bowl, mix the tomato paste with oregano and basil. Smear the paste over the chicken; place chicken into a baking dish. Season with salt and pepper.

3. Spread sliced olives over the chicken; top with diced tomatoes and onions. Sprinkle with red pepper flakes, if desired. Drizzle with olive oil.

4. Bake for 25-35 minutes.

Chicken Pesto
AVOCADO WRAPS

MEAT ▪ YIELDS 4 WRAPS

Since I'm not a cholent person, I'm always looking for recipes that I can serve cold on Shabbos day, and these chicken pesto avocado wraps have served me well! They're ideal for summer meals, and even the leftovers taste great for a light Motza'ei Shabbos dinner.

2	chicken breasts, skin on, on the bone
1 Tbsp	olive oil
▪	salt, to taste, divided
▪	pepper, to taste, divided
1	avocado, diced
1 cup	grape tomatoes, halved
1 cup	packed arugula
¼ cup	Spinach Pistachio Pesto (page 36) or store-bought pesto
¼ cup	mayonnaise
2 tsp	fresh-squeezed lemon juice
4	whole wheat wraps

1. Preheat oven to 400°F.

2. Place chicken into a baking pan. Drizzle with olive oil; season with salt and pepper.

3. Bake, uncovered, for 50 minutes. Remove the skin and bones from the chicken; using 2 forks, pull the chicken apart into shreds.

4. Add shredded chicken to a large bowl. Add avocado, tomatoes, arugula, pesto, mayonnaise, lemon juice, salt, and pepper. Toss together to combine.

5. Divide chicken mixture evenly between wraps, roll the wraps closed, and cut in half. Serve immediately or refrigerate until ready to serve.

VARIATION

For a carb-free option, serve the chicken salad on its own or in a roasted Portobello mushroom "bun."

NOTE

You may also use 2 grilled chicken breasts or 2 cups leftover shredded chicken.

Ma's Stuffed CORNISH HENS

MEAT ▪ YIELDS 4 SERVINGS ▪ FREEZER FRIENDLY

If I had to name my mom's signature dish, it would have to be her amazing Stuffed Cornish Hens. She makes them for every party, and we never get bored of them. Cornish hens make for beautiful presentation, but I often recreate this recipe with more basic chicken quarters or capons. This makes a great main dish for festive holiday dinners or sheva brachos.

4	Cornish hens
1 large (about 20-oz.)	challah, torn into chunks
10 oz.	frozen chopped spinach, thawed (1½ cups squeezed dry)
¼ cup	light olive oil
1½ cups	chicken stock, divided
1 tsp	poultry seasoning
▪	salt, to taste
▪	pepper, to taste
4 Tbsp	paprika
2 Tbsp	garlic powder
6 Tbsp	water
1 (15-oz.) bottle	sweet chili sauce

1. Preheat oven to 350°F.

2. Place the challah into a food processor; pulse until coarse crumbs forms.

3. Place the challah crumbs into a large bowl; add spinach, oil, 1 cup stock, and poultry seasoning. Season with salt and pepper.

4. Stuff the stuffing into the cavity of the Cornish hens.

5. In a small bowl, combine paprika, garlic powder, and 6 tablespoons water. Rub mixture all over the hens; season with salt and pepper. Place hens into 2 baking dishes. If there is any extra stuffing, place it in the dish alongside the chicken. Add ¼ cup remaining chicken stock (or water) to the bottom of each of the pans.

6. Cover tightly with foil; bake for 45 minutes-1 hour (depending on the size of your bird). Uncover; glaze hens with sweet chili sauce. Raise the oven temperature to 400 degrees and bake, uncovered, for 20-30 minutes.

—— VARIATIONS ——

Use 8 chicken quarters in place of the hens. Stuff the stuffing under the chicken skin and proceed as above. You may also use chicken capons (dark meat chicken cutlets). Fill 8 capons with the stuffing and seal closed with toothpicks. Proceed as above.

Curried Shake & Bake
DRUMSTICKS

MEAT ▪ YIELDS 6 SERVINGS

Those who follow me on Instagram will remember the breaded honey drumsticks that had a viral moment when I made them on my stories before Rosh Hashanah. The truth is, that was just my simplified version of the even better recipe that you'll find here. I was just saving the best for the book!

12	chicken drumsticks
1 cup	cornflake crumbs
3 tsp	paprika
1½ tsp	curry powder
1½ tsp	kosher salt
½ tsp	pepper
½ cup	honey

1. Preheat oven to 400°F. Line a baking sheet with foil; coat with nonstick cooking spray.

2. Place cornflake crumbs, paprika, curry powder, salt, and pepper into a large ziplock bag. Shake to distribute the spices.

3. Rinse drumsticks in cold water. Place each piece into the bag; shake to coat in crumbs.

4. Place coated drumsticks onto prepared baking sheet. Spray drumsticks generously with cooking spray.

5. Bake, uncovered, for 25 minutes. Drizzle honey onto drumsticks. Return pan to the oven; bake, uncovered, for 20 minutes.

NOTE

For best results, do not use a disposable baking sheet for this recipe.

VARIATION

To make the breaded honey drumsticks mentioned above, dip the chicken in flavored breadcrumbs. Continue with Step 4.

Braised Lemon Chicken
WITH LEEKS

MEAT · YIELDS 4 SERVINGS

Leeks are my vegetable of choice from the chicken soup; I love the silky texture and the mild oniony flavor. Most people don't think of leeks as a stand-alone vegetable, but they are delicious when braised with lemon and white wine. This simple recipe packs in the flavor and would make a great addition to your Pesach Seder.

2	leeks
1 Tbsp	olive oil
4	chicken legs
·	salt, to taste
·	pepper, to taste
2 large	shallots, thinly sliced
3 cloves	garlic, minced
½ cup	dry white wine
·	juice of 1 lemon
1	lemon, sliced
3	sprigs thyme

NOTE

If you don't have a Dutch oven, prepare Steps 3-4 in a frying pan, then transfer to a 9x13-inch roasting pan. Cover tightly with two layers of foil; continue as above.

1. Preheat oven to 350°F.

2. Trim both ends of the leeks; cut leeks in half lengthwise. Wash leeks under running water to remove dirt from between the layers. Pat dry; set aside.

3. Heat olive oil in a Dutch oven over medium heat. Season the chicken with salt and pepper; place skin-side down in the pan. Sear chicken until the skin is golden brown. Flip to sear second side. Remove from pan.

4. Add leeks to the pan; season with salt and pepper. Cook until they start to brown; flip to brown second side (it's OK if leeks come apart). Remove from the pan.

5. Add shallots and garlic to the pan; sauté until fragrant (add a small drizzle of olive oil, if needed). Pour wine into the pan; bring to a simmer, scraping up the bits from the bottom of the pan as it cooks.

6. Return leeks to the pan; add seared chicken. Squeeze lemon juice over the chicken; top with lemon slices and thyme. Cover; bake in the oven for 1 hour.

Maple Chili
SPATCHCOCK CHICKEN

MEAT ▪ YIELDS 4 SERVINGS

I make spatchcock chicken just so I can say the word! Spatchcock is the Millennial term for butterflying, and it's a great way to roast chicken because it cooks more evenly and makes for a beautiful presentation. This dish bakes on a single sheet tray, making it a 1-pan dinner with easy cleanup! Who doesn't love that?

1	whole chicken
½	butternut squash, peeled and cut into small chunks
1	Japanese sweet potato OR yam, peeled and cut into small chunks
2	carrots, peeled and cut into small chunks
1	red onion, peeled and cut into wedges
1 tsp	chili powder
1½ tsp	smoked paprika
¼ tsp	cinnamon
3 Tbsp	olive oil
¼ cup	maple syrup
▪	salt, to taste
▪	pepper, to taste

1. Preheat oven to 425°F. Line a baking sheet with parchment paper or foil.

2. **Spatchcock the chicken:** Place chicken on a cutting board, breast-side down. Starting at the thigh end, cut along one side of the backbone with kitchen shears. Turn chicken around; cut along the second side of the backbone. Discard backbone or freeze to use in chicken soup or stock.

3. Flip chicken over; open it like a book. Press firmly on the breastbone with your palms to flatten.

4. Spread chicken on a baking sheet. Arrange vegetables around chicken in a single layer. Sprinkle spices over chicken and vegetables; drizzle with olive oil and maple syrup. Season with salt and pepper.

5. Bake, uncovered, for 50-60 minutes, basting every 20 minutes with the pan juices.

— NOTE —

If it's hard to visualize, just google "how to spatchcock a chicken"; there are lots of tutorials you can follow — that's how I learned how to do it! You can also ask your butcher to butterfly the chicken for you, or just use chicken quarters instead.

Honey Roasted Za'atar Chicken
WITH DRIED FRUIT

MEAT ▪ YIELDS 4-6 SERVINGS ▪ FREEZER FRIENDLY

When I finally decided to take the cookbook plunge, my biggest challenge was figuring out which "best of the blog" recipes to feature — there are just so many! I'm proud to say that this recipe hooked hundreds of people onto the Middle Eastern spice blend, za'atar. I use it on pita chips, roasted chickpeas, hummus, shakshuka, and garlic confit.

10 oz.	dried apricots (scant 2 cups)
10 oz.	pitted dried prunes (scant 2 cups)
3 Tbsp	za'atar
2 Tbsp	olive oil
4	chicken legs, skin-on
½ cup	dry red wine
▪	salt, to taste
⅓ cup	honey

1. Preheat oven to 350°F. Spread apricots and prunes into a 9×13-inch pan.

2. In a bowl, combine za'atar and olive oil to create a paste. Rub the za'atar paste over chicken; place chicken on dried fruit. Pour wine around the chicken; sprinkle with salt.

3. Cover tightly with foil; bake for 1 hour.

4. Uncover the pan. Drizzle the chicken with honey. Bake, uncovered, for an additional 30-45 minutes, basting every 10 minutes with the pan juices.

Fennel & Orange Turkey Roast
WITH CAPERS

MEAT ▪ YIELDS 6-8 SERVINGS ▪ FREEZER FRIENDLY

Fennel has been growing on me. I was never really a fan of the anise flavor, but I've found that it greatly diminishes upon roasting. Shaving the fennel thinly on a mandolin also works to mellow the strong licorice taste, but roasting has become my preferred method of preparation. In this recipe, the unique pairing of the fennel, marmalade, capers, and wine work surprisingly well together and keep the turkey moist and flavorful.

½ cup	orange marmalade
2 cloves	garlic, minced
2 sprigs	fresh rosemary, roughly chopped
1 Tbsp	caper brine
1 (2.5-lb.)	turkey roast
▪	salt, to taste
▪	pepper, to taste
1 large or 2 medium	fennel bulb(s)
1 Tbsp	capers
2 Tbsp	olive oil
¼ cup	dry white wine

1. Preheat oven to 350°F. In a small bowl, combine marmalade, garlic, rosemary, and caper brine. Brush the mixture over the turkey roast and season with salt and pepper. Place into a baking dish.

2. Trim fronds from fennel bulbs; discard fronds. Slice fennel bulb in half lengthwise; cut each half into thin slices. Place fennel slices into the baking dish around the turkey; season with salt and pepper.

3. Sprinkle capers over roast; drizzle olive oil over the pan. Pour the wine around the turkey.

4. Bake, covered, for 1 hour. Uncover, raise the oven temperature to 400°F, and bake until the internal temperature reads 165°F, about 35 minutes.

MEAT

Guide to KOSHER MEAT COOKERY

Over the years, I have found that kosher meat cookery is vastly misunderstood, and for good reason. There are so many cuts of meat, with different names and cooking methods. I set out to clarify the confusion with a meat guide on my blog, and it's one of my most popular features to date. I couldn't imagine not including it here as well!

Where does the meat that we eat actually come from?

The different cuts of meat that you buy at the butcher typically come from a steer. The steer is cut up into 9 sections, or PRIMAL CUTS, 5 of which are used for kosher consumption in the United States. The chuck/shoulder, rib, brisket, plate, and foreshank are cut into subprimals or fabricated cuts, which is what you typically see at the supermarket or butcher shop.

To succeed in cooking beef, the key is to understand where on the animal the actual cut comes from. Meat is made up of muscle and connective tissue. The more a muscle is used, the more connective tissue it will have, causing the meat to be tough.

Why does it matter where our meat comes from?

Once we understand the nature of the meat (whether it's tough or tender), we can determine what type of cooking method it requires. Tough cuts of meat require moist cooking to break down the muscle fibers and connective tissues. Tender cuts benefit from dry heat cooking to firm up the meat without breaking down connective tissue.

FABRICATED CUTS

Here's where things get tricky. Kosher butchers (and butchers in general) tend to name their cuts whatever they like. You can find the same cut of meat with two different names, depending on where you shop. That said, these are some of the most popular fabricated cuts that you'll find:

- **CHUCK/SHOULDER:**

    Chuck roast: *Often sold tied in a net, this cut includes* **chuck eye roast, square roast, brick roast, California roast,** *and* **French roast**. *The names are often interchangeable, and any roast may be used in a recipe that calls for braising. The exception is the* **Delmonico or club roast**, *a tender cut from the end of the chuck, right near the ribs. It is often sliced into*

club steaks and benefits from dry heat cooking. (Some butchers use boneless rib eye for this cut.)

    Kolichol: *Great to use in the cholent or wherever a recipe calls for pot roast.*

    Minute (Steak) Roast: *Easily identified by the thick piece of gristle that runs down the center, this is a delicious roast that needs to be braised. When the roast is sliced horizontally above and below the gristle, the resulting cut is known as the flatiron steak, filet split, or minute London broil; it's perfect for stir fry or wherever recipes call for quick grilling.*

    Shoulder London Broil *or Shoulder Steaks: This is a lean cut that should be grilled or broiled. It is best served rare and sliced thin. (I prefer the shoulder blade, A.K.A. butcher's cut.)*

    Silver Tip Roast: *Used to make roast beef. Benefits from dry heat cooking.*

- **RIBS:** Ribs are the most tender cut of kosher meat because the muscles in this area are not worked as much. Ribs should always be cooked using a dry heat cooking method. The rib section includes **rib steaks, ribeye steaks, mock filet mignon,** and **back ribs**. There is also a great cut known as the **surprise** or **crescent steak** — a flap that covers the prime rib and is tender and delicious. Above the surprise steak is the **top of the rib,** the one exception to the rule of the rib section. The top of the rib is a tougher cut and benefits from moist heat cooking.

    There are three types of beef ribs, each from a different part of the steer. **Back ribs** are from the rib primal, and are the ribs you'd see on a bone-in rib steak. There is not a lot of meat on the back ribs (known as finger meat) but it is tender and flavorful. Back ribs are best smoked for 4-5 hours, or slow-cooked in foil and then roasted or broiled.

    The 5 ribs from the chuck are generally called **flanken** or **5-bone ribs**. They are leaner than the plate ribs, A.K.A. short ribs, which come from the belly. Flanken ribs are typically cut across the 5 bones in 2-3-inch-wide strips. They are great for stews and soups or saucy dishes.

Plate or **short ribs** are significantly fattier than flanken, and are great for smoking or grilling. The plate ribs can be cut in 2-3" strips across the (3) bones like flanken, or be cut in half to make smaller 4-5" racks. When left whole, they are sometimes called "dinosaur" ribs since they can be 8-12" long. When the ribs are cut in into individual pieces along the bone, they are known as **spare ribs**.

- **PLATE:** The plate sits below the rib primal and contains the short ribs and the "beef belly" that is either used for making beef fry or pastrami. It also includes the flavorful **skirt** and **hanger steaks**. Both have a high salt content and benefit from quick grilling. I prefer to soak these steaks in water for about 1 hour to draw out some of the salt before grilling.

- **BRISKET:** Brisket is the breast of the steer and is an extremely tough cut. Brisket is often sold as 1st and 2nd cut. First cut brisket is flat. It is much less flavorful than the second cut, which is smaller but fattier. Fat is flavorful, so when possible, always opt for a well-marbled cut over a leaner one. You can always refrigerate the cooked meat and remove the congealed fat later on.

  First cut brisket tends to cut nicely, while second cut tends to shred, making it perfect for pulled beef. Corned beef and pastrami are often made from brisket. Corned beef is pickled, while pastrami is pickled and then smoked.

- **FORESHANK:** The foreshank is very flavorful and high in collagen. It includes the shin and marrow bones. Which are often cross-cut for osso bucco. Because collagen converts to gelatin when cooked using moist heat, shanks are excellent for making stocks and bone broth.

- **ADDITIONAL PARTS:** In addition to the primal cuts of the animal, there are other edible parts of the steer, including the neck (mostly used ground up due to its connective tissues), cheek (great for braising), sweetbreads (thymus gland), liver, tongue, and oxtails (hard to find kosher due to the complications involved in removing the forbidden fats and veins).

- **GROUND BEEF:** Ground beef can come from any part of the animal, but it is usually made from lean cuts and trimmings. When purchasing ground beef, keep in mind that the leaner the meat, the drier your end product will be. 80% lean to 20% fat is a good ratio.

PASTURE RAISED & GRASSFED MEAT

How an animal is raised will affect how it tastes. Cattle in the United States are usually finished in feedlots on a diet that is very high in grains, antibiotics, and hormones in order to fatten them up and keep them from getting sick. Animals raised in these conditions tend to be less healthy, whereas meat from animals raised outdoors on pasture are healthier and their meat is more flavorful. Meat from grass-fed cattle is extremely lean, so it's important not to overcook it. Ask your meat purveyor for suggested cooking times, depending on the cut. A great source for high-quality pastured kosher meats in America is Grow & Behold Foods (www.growandbehold.com).

COOKING METHODS

- **Dry Heat Cooking:** Includes broiling, grilling, roasting, and pan-searing. Meat should be cooked at high temperatures to caramelize the surface. To determine doneness, check the temperature with a meat thermometer.

  Temperatures: **VERY RARE:** 120-125°, **RARE** (deep red center) 125-130°, **MEDIUM RARE** (bright red center) 130-140°, **MEDIUM** (pink center) 140-150°, **MEDIUM WELL** (very little pink) 155-165°, **WELL DONE** (all brown) 165°+.

- **CARRYOVER COOKING**: When meat has finished cooking and is removed from the heat, the internal temperature will continue to rise by about 10 degrees. Therefore, keep in mind carryover cooking when using dry heat cooking methods and remove your meat from the heat source 10 degrees below your desired temperature.

- **MOIST HEAT COOKING:** Includes simmering (used for corned beef and tongue) and braising or stewing.

- Braised meats are first browned and then cooked in a small amount of liquid. Wine and/or tomatoes are often used, as the acid helps to break down and tenderize the meat. To determine doneness when braising or stewing, you do not need a thermometer; just use a fork to check for tenderness.

- **SOUS VIDE COOKING:** *Sous vide* means "under vacuum" and it is a method of cooking vacuum-sealed food in a temperature-controlled water bath for gentle, slow cooking. Sous vide is especially beneficial for cooking meat because the cooking process tenderizes cheaper cuts and offers superior, even, and precise results.

RESTING & CUTTING MEAT

When meat has finished cooking, it's always important to let it rest 10-20 minutes before slicing. Resting allows the juices to redistribute themselves, and cutting into the meat too early will cause all the juices to run out onto your cutting board or platter.

As mentioned, meat is a group of muscle fibers that band together to form muscles. When cutting meat, it's important to cut against the grain (perpendicular to the muscle fibers) in order to shorten the muscle fibers so that they are more tender. Cutting parallel to the muscle fibers results in chewy, stringy cuts of meat.

Hasselback Salami
THREE WAYS

MEAT ▪ YIELDS 6-8 SERVINGS EACH

Drunken Hasselback Salami is the recipe that put Busy in Brooklyn on the map. It's my most viral recipe of all time, with versions spanning the globe, at deli counters and Jewish households worldwide. I knew the classic version had to go in the book, but I wanted to gift you with two other variations, plus a fun way of serving up this crowd-pleasing dish.

See photo on following page.

DRUNKEN HASSELBACK SALAMI

½ cup	apricot jam
¼ cup	spicy brown mustard
3 Tbsp	brandy or bourbon
2 Tbsp	ketchup
1 Tbsp	brown sugar
1 (16-oz.)	salami

1. Preheat oven to 400°F.

2. Add all ingredients except salami to a pot; whisk over medium heat until jam is melted and mixture begins to boil and thicken.

3. Remove wrapping from salami. Place salami on a cutting board with chopsticks on either side. Holding the salami with one hand, slice into thin, even slices. (The chopsticks will ensure that you don't slice all the way through. See page 170)

4. Place salami into a baking pan. Generously brush salami with the sauce, making sure to get it between all the slices. Bake, uncovered, for approximately 45 minutes, basting every 10-15 minutes, until the salami is browned and crispy around the edges. Serve warm with any remaining sauce for dipping.

CRISPY BREADED SALAMI

1 (16 oz.)	salami
1½ cups	french fried onions, crushed
½ cup	panko breadcrumbs
½ tsp	smoked paprika
½ cup	barbecue sauce

1. Preheat oven to 350°F.

2. Remove wrapping from salami. Place salami on a cutting board with chopsticks on either side. Holding the salami with one hand, slice into thin, even slices. (The chopsticks will ensure that you don't slice all the way through. See page 170)

3. In a small bowl, combine crushed onions, panko, and smoked paprika.

4. Smear barbecue sauce over salami, coating between the slices. Coat the salami in the onion mixture, taking care to stuff it between and around the slices.

5. Bake, uncovered, for 30-40 minutes or until the coating starts to brown.

CRANBERRY GLAZED HASSELBACK SALAMI

1 cup	cranberry sauce
2 tsp	sriracha
2 cloves	garlic, crushed
2 Tbsp	rice vinegar
4 tsp	soy sauce
1 (16-oz.)	salami

1. Preheat oven to 400°F.

2. Add all ingredients except salami to a pot; whisk over medium heat until cranberry sauce is melted and mixture begins to boil and thicken.

3. Remove wrapping from salami. Place salami on a cutting board with chopsticks on either side. Holding the salami with one hand, slice into thin, even slices. (The chopsticks will ensure that you don't slice all the way through. See page 170)

4. Place salami into a baking pan. Generously brush salami with the sauce, making sure to get it between all the slices. Bake, uncovered, for approximately 45 minutes, basting every 10-15 minutes, until the salami is browned and crispy around the edges. Serve warm with any remaining sauce for dipping.

HOW TO BUILD A CHARCUTERIE BOARD

To build a charcuterie board (see photo on following page), you don't need a recipe, just a basic outline of components.

Using the following suggestions as inspiration, build your board by arranging assorted meats, breads, fruit, nuts, pickles, and condiments on a rustic platter or board.

Lay the meats out first around the board; swirl the crackers and fruits around it.

Fill the empty spaces with small bowls of nuts, pickles, olives, and condiments.

Have fun with it and let your creative spirit guide you!

- **Meats:**
  - hasselback salami
  - cured and dried sausages and meats
  - jerky
  - smoked turkey
  - pâté
  - cocktail meatballs
  - kofta-stuffed dates
  - franks in blanks

- **Bread & Crackers:**
  - sliced baguette
  - crostini
  - crackers
  - breadsticks

- **Fruits & Vegetables:**
  - pears
  - persimmon
  - grapes
  - dried dates
  - dried apricots
  - dried figs
  - tomatoes on the vine

- **Nuts and Seeds:**
  - sunflower seeds
  - cashews
  - pistachios
  - pecans
  - almonds

- **Pickles and Olives:**
  - pickled onions
  - cornichons
  - Kalamata and other olives

- **Condiments:**
  - assorted mustards
  - fig jam
  - honey
  - hot pepper jam
  - tapenade

Beer-Marinated London Broil
WITH ARUGULA CHIMICHURRI

MEAT • YIELDS 6 SERVINGS

London broil is the cut of meat that I purchase most often. It's budget friendly, and cooks up super quickly. Technically, London broil is not an actual cut, but rather a cooking method: Marinating and then grilling or broiling for optimum tenderness. Most kosher London broil is cut from the shoulder, and I prefer the shoulder blade cut. While thin, the cut is extremely tender and flavorful, especially when marinated in beer.

2 cloves	garlic, minced
1 tsp	cumin
½ tsp	chili powder
½ tsp	oregano
2 Tbsp	olive oil
1 (2-lb.)	London broil, shoulder blade cut preferred
1 cup	beer
•	juice of 1 lime
1 Tbsp	honey
•	salt, to taste
•	pepper, to taste

ARUGULA CHIMICHURRI

1 cup	arugula
2 cloves	garlic
½ tsp	red pepper flakes
2	scallions
•	juice of 1 lime
1 tsp	oregano
2 Tbsp	red wine vinegar
½ cup	olive oil
•	salt to taste
•	pepper to taste

1. In a small bowl, combine garlic, cumin, chili powder, oregano, and olive oil. Rub the spice mixture over the London broil and place into a ziplock bag. Add beer, lime juice, and honey; seal bag. Marinate the meat in the refrigerator for 3 hours or up to overnight.

2. Remove meat from marinade; pat dry. Discard marinade. Place meat into a pan. Bring meat to room temperature for 20 minutes while you preheat grill or broiler. Season with salt and pepper. Grill or broil on high for 6-8 minutes per side (or 8-10 for the thicker shoulder cut) or until desired doneness is reached.

3. Allow meat to rest for 10 minutes; slice thinly against the grain.

4. **Prepare the arugula chimichurri:** Add chimichurri ingredients to a food processor or blender; blend until smooth, scraping down the sides as needed. Serve with London broil.

SOUS VIDE OPTION

Remove meat from the marinade and place into a ziplock bag. Using the water displacement method, place into a water bath set to 129°F (or temperature of choice). Cook for one hour (for a 1-inch-thick London broil; increase to 2 hours for a 2-inch-thick cut). Remove meat from the bag; pat dry thoroughly. Season with salt and pepper; sear over high heat on each side. Slice thinly against the grain.

USES

You can also serve the chimichurri with grilled chicken or steak.

NOTE

If preparing in advance, bring to room temperature before serving. Do not warm.

Sticky Silan
SHORT RIBS

MEAT ▪ YIELDS 6 SERVINGS ▪ FREEZER FRIENDLY

Short ribs are not something I make every day. They can be pricey and I like to reserve them for special occasions. I developed this recipe with Rosh Hashanah in mind, smothering the ribs in a sticky coating of date honey for a sweet New Year.

3 lbs.	short ribs
1 batch	Sweet and Smoky Spice Rub (recipe below)
½ cup	silan
1 cup	pomegranate seeds
▪	handful of parsley, roughly chopped
▪	Parsnip Puree (page 238), for serving, optional

1. Preheat oven to 325°F. Rub the spice mix generously over the ribs.

2. Place the ribs into a 9x13-inch pan with the fat side facing up. Cover tightly with 2 layers of foil; bake for 3 hours, until ribs are tender and falling off the bone.

3. Remove the ribs from the oven; raise oven temperature to 425°F. Discard most of the juices from the pan, leaving about ½ cup. Drizzle the ribs generously with silan and bake, uncovered, for 15 minutes, basting every 5 minutes with silan from the pan.

4. To serve, garnish with pomegranate seeds and fresh parsley. Serve with parsnip puree, if desired.

SWEET & SMOKY SPICE RUB

3 Tbsp	brown sugar
2 Tbsp	smoked paprika
1 Tbsp	cumin
1 Tbsp	kosher salt
1½ tsp	pepper
1 tsp	allspice
½ tsp	cinnamon

▪ Combine all ingredients in a small bowl; mix well.

Fall Harvest
APPLE & HONEY ROAST

MEAT • YIELDS 6-8 SERVINGS • FREEZER FRIENDLY

At the local grocery store where I shop, Klara Gottesman manages the meat department. She is the sweetest lady I've ever met — always showering me with compliments and telling me how proud she is of my work. Klara knows her cuts of meat, and whenever I'm not sure where a specific cut comes from, she is always quick to answer. I love to chat with her about food and exchange recipes and ideas. One year, before Rosh Hashanah, Klara shared her festive apple roast recipe with me, and I've been making this adapted version ever since.

SPICE RUB

2 Tbsp	paprika
1 Tbsp	garlic powder
1 tsp	oregano
2 tsp	kosher salt
1 tsp	pepper
3 Tbsp	canola oil

ROAST

1 (3-4-lb.)	roast
3 Tbsp	canola oil
1 large	onion, peeled and sliced into half-moons
4 cloves	garlic, minced
1 cup	apple cider
1 cup	dry red wine
1 lb.	lady apples (NOT Pink Lady)
¼ cup	honey
•	salt, to taste
•	pepper, to taste

1. Preheat oven to 325°F.

2. **Prepare the spice rub:** In a small bowl, combine the paprika, garlic powder, oregano, salt, and pepper. Add 3 tablespoons canola oil; mix to combine.

3. **Prepare the roast:** Brush spice rub over the roast, covering it on all sides. Heat oil in a Dutch oven; sear the roast over medium heat, taking care not to burn the spices, until browned on all sides. Remove meat from the pot.

4. Add onions to the pan; sauté until translucent. Add garlic; sauté until fragrant. Add apple cider and red wine; bring the mixture to a boil over high heat, scraping up the bits from the bottom of the pan.

5. Return the meat to the pan; place the apples around it. Drizzle honey over the roast. Season with salt and pepper. Cover; place into the oven. Cook, for 90 minutes. Turn roast; roast for another 90 minutes, or until fork tender.

NOTE

This recipe can be adapted to use many cuts of beef including chuck eye roast, French roast, square roast, and minute steak roast.

TIP

If you don't have a Dutch oven, prepare steps 3-4 in a frying pan, then transfer to a 9x13-inch roasting pan. Cover tightly with two layers of foil; continue as above.

FREEZING INSTRUCTIONS

When roast is completely cool, cut into slices against the grain. Double wrap the sliced roast in foil; label and freeze. Pour the sauce (with the apples) into a large container; label and freeze. The night before you're ready to serve, transfer frozen roast and sauce to the refrigerator. Before serving, place the sliced roast into a pot or pan and pour defrosted sauce over it. Heat on the stovetop or in the oven until heated through.

Tuscan
VEAL CHOPS

MEAT • YIELDS 2 SERVINGS

I'm always looking for beef alternatives and veal is just the thing — it's tender, sweeter, and much lighter than beef. Veal chops are easy to cook and make an elegant date-night dinner. While I love going out to eat, there's something nice about staying home and cooking up a special meal, so pick up a nice bottle of white wine and stay in for a change.

2	veal chops (about ¾-inch thick)
¼ cup	flour
1 tsp	herbes de Provence, optional
•	salt, to taste
•	pepper, to taste
2 Tbsp	olive oil
1 large or 2 small	shallot(s), thinly sliced
2 cloves	garlic, minced
1 cup	halved grape tomatoes
⅓ cup	white wine
1 cup	vegetable stock
1 Tbsp	whole grain mustard
10	basil leaves, chiffonade
•	salt, to taste
•	pepper, to taste

1. In a shallow dish, combine flour, herbes de Provence, salt, and pepper. Lightly dredge the veal chops in the flour mixture, shaking off the excess.

2. In a large frying pan, heat oil over medium heat. Fry the veal chops until golden brown on both sides and set aside, tenting with foil to keep warm.

3. Add shallots and garlic to the pan; sauté until fragrant. Add tomatoes; sauté until the tomatoes soften and begin to release their juices, about 3 minutes. Add wine; simmer until reduced by half, scraping up the bits from the bottom of the pan as it cooks.

4. Add stock; cook until reduced by half. Add mustard and basil; stir to combine. Season, to taste, with salt and pepper.

5. Add veal chops to the pan; warm in the sauce. Serve immediately.

— NOTE —

You may also prepare this recipe using veal cutlets or veal scaloppini.

— TIP —

To chiffonade basil, stack the leaves and then roll up the stack. Slice the roll into thin ribbons.

Crockpot
BBQ PULLED BEEF

MEAT ▪ YIELDS 10-12 SERVINGS ▪ FREEZER FRIENDLY

This crockpot BBQ beef was originally named my Blogoversary BBQ Brisket (can you tell I love alliteration?) because I made it to celebrate the third anniversary of my blog. It has since become a family favorite for followers worldwide.

1 (3-lb.)	second cut brisket
▪	salt, to taste
▪	pepper, to taste
2 Tbsp	olive oil
1 large	onion, sliced into half-moons
4 cloves	garlic, minced
1 cup	ketchup
1 cup	apple cider vinegar
1 cup	packed brown sugar
1 Tbsp	smoked paprika
1 Tbsp	sweet paprika
2 cups	chicken stock

1. Sprinkle brisket with salt and pepper. Heat the oil in a deep skillet over medium-high heat; sear the brisket on all sides. Place the brisket into a crockpot.

2. In the same skillet, sauté onions until translucent. Add garlic; continue to sauté until fragrant. Add the ketchup, vinegar, brown sugar, smoked and Hungarian paprika, and chicken stock. Bring the mixture to a boil; reduce for 20 minutes to create a sauce.

3. Pour sauce over the brisket. Turn the crockpot on to high. Slow cook for 5-6 hours, until meat is tender.

4. Remove brisket from the crockpot. Using 2 forks, pull the meat into shreds. Pour the sauce into a pan; reduce until thick (it should coat the back of a spoon), 20-30 minutes.

5. Return the shredded beef to the crockpot; pour thickened sauce over meat. Stir to coat meat. Set the crockpot to warm or serve immediately.

—— SERVING SUGGESTIONS ——

Tacos: *Serve with Red Cabbage Slaw (page 143), pomegranate seeds, and Quick Pickled Onions page 22).*

Sliders: *Serve with coleslaw and pickled jalapeños.*

Nachos: *Serve over tortilla chips with guacamole, pico de gallo or salsa, and nondairy sour cream.*

Other suggestions: *Serve over mashed potatoes or stuff into baked potatoes, egg rolls, or bourekas.*

—— NOTE ——

To prepare for a Shabbos day meal, omit steps 4 and 5; cook on low until ready to serve.

Lazy Mechshie
MEATBALLS

MEAT ▪ YIELDS 6 SERVINGS

Mechshie is to my husband what stuffed cabbage is to me — the food of his youth. While my Ashkenazi mother was stuffing cabbage leaves with meat and rice, his Syrian mother was stuffing zucchini and tomatoes with hashu. I love preparing mechshie for my family too, but the tedious process of hollowing out the vegetables can be time-consuming. This is my lazy version: all of the flavor, less of the prep.

MEATBALLS

1 lb.	ground meat
⅓ cup	rice (I prefer basmati)
2 Tbsp	grated onion
½ tsp	allspice
1 tsp	kosher salt
¼ tsp	pepper
2 Tbsp	water

SAUCE

2 (15-oz.) cans	tomato sauce
½ cup	brown sugar
1 tsp	allspice
1 tsp	kosher salt
▪	juice of ½ lemon
½ cup	diced dried apricots
1½ cups	shredded zucchini
1 cup	water

FOR SERVING

▪	prepared zoodles or rice

1. **Prepare the sauce:** In a saucepan, combine tomato sauce, brown sugar, allspice, salt, lemon, apricots, zucchini, and water. Bring the mixture to a boil; reduce to a simmer.

2. **Meanwhile, prepare the meatballs:** In a bowl, combine meat, rice, onion, allspice, salt, pepper and water. Roll the mixture into small balls; drop into the simmering sauce. Simmer for 1 hour, or until meatballs are tender.

3. Serve with zoodles or rice.

Empanada ROLL

MEAT • YIELDS 12 SERVINGS • FREEZER FRIENDLY

Raised in Argentina, my mother-in-law adopted many South American dishes that she brought with her to America and fused with her Syrian heritage. My kids love her beef and olive empanadas, but since I don't usually have the time to fold and twist individual servings, I came up with this quick deli roll version using frozen puff pastry.

1 Tbsp	olive oil
1 medium	onion, peeled and diced
2 cloves	garlic, minced
1 lb.	ground beef
1 Tbsp	cumin
2 tsp	smoked paprika
1 tsp	chili powder
½ tsp	dried oregano
▪	salt, to taste
▪	pepper, to taste
½ cup	pimento-stuffed olives, chopped
1 cup	water
2 Tbsp	cornstarch mixed with 2 Tbsp water
2 sheets	puff pastry, thawed in the refrigerator overnight
1	egg, beaten with 1 Tbsp water, for egg wash
2 Tbsp	sesame seeds

1. Heat olive oil in a deep skillet over medium heat. Add onion, sauté until translucent. Add garlic; sauté until fragrant. Add ground beef; cook until no longer pink, breaking it up as it cooks. Drain the juices from the skillet.

2. Add the spices; stir until meat is coated. Add olives; stir to incorporate. Add water; bring to a simmer. Add cornstarch mixture. Simmer until the mixture is thick and bubbly, about 5 minutes.

3. When you are ready to assemble the rolls, preheat oven to 400°F. Line a baking sheet with parchment paper.

4. Remove puff pastry from the fridge. Lay 1 sheet of pastry on prepared baking sheet; roll it out lightly. Place half the meat filling onto the center of the pastry; fold both sides over so they meet in the middle. Pinch the dough closed; fold over the ends to seal. Use parchment paper liner to roll the log over so that the seam is on the bottom. Repeat with the second sheet of dough and filling.

5. Cut a few horizontal slits along the length of each roll; brush with egg wash. Sprinkle with sesame seeds; bake for 25-30 minutes, until puffed and golden. Slice and serve warm.

───── VARIATION ─────

You may prepare individual servings using puff pastry squares.

───── QUICK & EASY ─────

For a quick and easy version, prepare ground beef using store-bought taco seasoning. Add chopped olives; fill the puff pastry as per above instructions.

Lamb Moussaka
EGGPLANT "BOATS"

MEAT • YIELDS 4-6 SERVINGS • FREEZER FRIENDLY

Deconstructing recipes is a fun challenge for me, especially so when it comes to eggplant (hence my Eggplant Boats staple recipe!). I have wanted to master deconstructed moussaka for a long time, but my biggest obstacle was what to do about the béchamel. Moussaka is traditionally smothered in the classic dairy sauce that's used in mac 'n cheese, but that's not allowed in kosher moussaka. I came up with the idea of making a cauliflower cream instead. I'm super proud of this one!

MEAT SAUCE

2 Tbsp	olive oil
1 large	onion, peeled and diced
3 cloves	garlic, minced
2 lbs.	ground lamb OR beef
1 (14.5-oz.) can	diced tomatoes
2 Tbsp	tomato paste
½ cup	dry red wine
1	bay leaf
¼ tsp	cinnamon
½ tsp	allspice
•	salt, to taste
•	pepper, to taste

CAULIFLOWER BÉCHAMEL

16 oz.	frozen cauliflower
1 clove	garlic
½ cup	unsweetened refrigerated almond milk OR vegetable stock
1 Tbsp	nutritional yeast
1	egg yolk
•	salt, to taste
•	pepper, to taste

FOR SERVING

4	Roasted Eggplant Boats, prepared according to instructions on page 38
•	fresh parsley, for garnish

1. **Prepare the meat sauce:** In a deep skillet, heat the olive oil. Add onion; sauté until translucent. Add garlic; sauté until fragrant. Add ground lamb; sauté until no longer pink, breaking it up as it cooks. Drain fat from the pan.

2. Add diced tomatoes, tomato paste, red wine, bay leaf, cinnamon, allspice, salt, and pepper. Bring the mixture to a boil. Reduce heat; simmer for 15 minutes. Discard bay leaf.

3. **Meanwhile, prepare the cauliflower béchamel:** Add cauliflower and garlic to a pot of salted water; bring to a boil. Cook until tender, 10-15 minutes; drain well. Add almond milk, nutritional yeast, egg yolk, salt, and pepper. Puree with an immersion blender until creamy.

4. Preheat oven to 350°F. Divide the meat sauce between the prepared eggplant boats; top with cauliflower béchamel. Bake for 10-15 minutes. Garnish with fresh parsley.

VARIATION

You can also prepare this recipe by layering broiled eggplant, meat sauce, and cauliflower puree in an oven-to-table casserole dish; bake at 350°F until the cauliflower is set. Alternatively, omit eggplant boats; serve meat sauce over rice or mashed potatoes.

MEATLESS MEALS

Tempeh Fajita Lettuce Cups

Mushroom Barley Risotto

Fully Loaded Stuffed Eggplant

Crockpot Moroccan Vegetable Stew

Refried Bean Tacos

Broccoli Burgers

Quinoa Pad Thai Bowls

Vegetarian Chili

Tempeh
FAJITA LETTUCE CUPS

PAREVE ▪ YIELDS 4-6 SERVINGS

I'm new to the tempeh train, I must admit, but I'm enjoying the ride. I was never a fan of tofu, because I'm all about texture, and tempeh delivers. With bits of crunchy soybeans, tempeh has a nice bite to it; it's firmer than tofu and provides more of a chew. If you're hesitant to try it, you can also make these lettuce cups with diced chicken or even pepper steak.

1 (8-oz.) package	tempeh, cut into cubes
½ cup	salsa (preferably smooth)
▪	juice of 1 lime
2 tsp	cumin, divided
3 Tbsp	olive oil, divided
▪	salt, to taste
▪	pepper, to taste
1 large	Spanish onion, sliced into half moons
½	red pepper
½	green pepper
½	orange pepper
1 tsp	smoked paprika
2 tsp	chili powder
▪	Boston lettuce, or lettuce of choice, for serving
▪	sliced avocado, for serving
▪	lime wedges, for serving

SALSA CREMA

½ cup	salsa of choice
½ cup	nondairy sour cream OR mayonnaise

1. Place tempeh, salsa, lime juice, and 1 teaspoon cumin into a ziplock bag; marinate for a few hours or overnight.

2. Heat 1 tablespoon olive oil in a wok or skillet; add the tempeh and salsa from the bag. Add salt and pepper to taste. Sauté the tempeh until it starts to brown and the salsa thickens into a glaze. Remove from the pan.

3. Add remaining 2 tablespoons olive oil. Add onion; sauté until translucent. Add peppers; continue to sauté until softened. Add smoked paprika, chili powder, remaining cumin, and salt. Sauté until the vegetables are coated and fragrant. Return tempeh to the pan; stir to incorporate.

4. **Prepare the salsa crema:** In a small bowl, combine salsa with nondairy sour cream.

5. To serve, separate lettuce leaves into cups; fill with fajita mixture. Add avocado slices; drizzle with salsa crema. Serve with lime wedges.

Mushroom Barley
RISOTTO

PAREVE ▪ YIELDS 6 SERVINGS ▪ FREEZER FRIENDLY

My crockpot mushroom barley soup is one of the most popular soups/stews on my blog. It's my daughter's favorite dish and it's the one I make whenever I'm cooking dinner for a family because it's such a crowd pleaser. There's just something about the barley that makes the soup ethereally creamy, and I realized I could use that to my benefit. You see, I love risotto. What I don't enjoy is standing over the pot, stirring in ladle after ladle of stock to make the classic dish. Here, I let the barley do the thickening, and with little effort, you're left with the creamiest bowl of comfort food that really hits the spot, even without the meat. My mushroom barley-loving kid approves!

2 Tbsp	olive oil
1 medium	onion, diced small
2 cloves	garlic, minced
10 oz.	cremini mushrooms, stems removed
3.5 oz.	oyster mushrooms, stems removed
3.5 oz.	shiitake mushrooms, stems removed
½ cup	dry white wine
1 cup	barley, rinsed
1 Tbsp	soy sauce
4	sprigs thyme
1	bay leaf
8 cups	vegetable stock
▪	salt, to taste
▪	pepper, to taste
▪	white truffle oil, for finishing

1. Heat a 5-quart stock pot over medium heat. Add olive oil. Add onion; sauté until translucent. Add garlic; sauté until fragrant.

2. Slice mushrooms; add to pot. Cook until softened and most of the liquid has evaporated. Add wine; cook until most of the liquid is absorbed.

3. Add barley, soy sauce, thyme, bay leaf, and stock; bring to a boil. Lower heat to medium; simmer with the cover half off until barley is tender and the risotto is creamy, with a porridge consistency, stirring occasionally, about 1 hour. Season, to taste, with salt and pepper.

4. To serve, discard bay leaf and thyme sprigs; divide risotto between serving bowls. Finish with a drizzle of truffle oil.

— VARIATION —

For dairy meals, add Parmesan cheese to taste. For meat meals, use beef stock in place of vegetable stock.

Fully Loaded
STUFFED EGGPLANT

PAREVE • YIELDS 4 SERVINGS

I can eat fully loaded stuffed eggplants every day of the week and never get bored. I love that I can fancy it up with homemade falafel, or go the easy route with the frozen stuff (or falafel-spiced chickpeas!). It's the ultimate Israeli comfort food, without the pita — all the glory minus the guilt!

4	prepared Roasted Eggplant Boats (page 38)
⅓ cup	Hummus (page 66)
•	Red Cabbage Slaw (page 143)
•	Israeli Salad (at right)
4	Israeli pickles, thinly sliced
12	frozen falafel balls, prepared according to package directions OR Falafel Roasted Chickpeas (page 304)
1 cup	Tahini (page 26)
•	harissa, optional, to taste

1. Coat eggplant boats with hummus.

2. Top with red cabbage slaw, Israeli salad, Israeli pickles, falafel balls, tahini, and harissa.

ISRAELI SALAD

2	plum tomatoes
1	English cucumber
½	red onion
1 Tbsp	olive oil
•	juice of ½ lemon
•	salt, to taste
•	pepper, to taste
•	fresh parsley, to taste

1. Finely dice tomatoes, cucumber, and onion. Drizzle with olive oil and lemon juice; season with salt and pepper.

2. Garnish with fresh parsley or chop parsley finely and add to salad.

Crockpot
MOROCCAN VEGETABLE STEW

PAREVE · YIELDS 8 SERVINGS

I'm not a cholent person. There, I said it. It just doesn't appeal to me. It's my husband's job to make it every week, and he likes to get creative, playing around with different combinations. Me, on the other hand, I prefer lighter vegetable stews like this Moroccan version. It's sweet, comforting, and doesn't leave you feeling like you need a nap. My kind of dinner.

2 Tbsp	olive oil
1 medium	onion, diced
3 cloves	garlic, minced
1 tsp	turmeric
1 tsp	coriander
½ tsp	cinnamon
½ tsp	cumin
¼ tsp	nutmeg
¼ tsp	chili powder
4 cups	vegetable stock
1 small	butternut squash, cut into chunks
2 medium	zucchini, cut into chunks
2	carrots, cut into chunks
1 small	sweet potato, cut into chunks
12 oz.	fresh or frozen cauliflower
1 can	chickpeas, drained and rinsed
½ cup	golden raisins
▪	salt, to taste
▪	pepper, to taste
2 cups	couscous, prepared according to package directions
▪	fresh parsley, for garnish
▪	sliced almonds, toasted, for garnish

1. In a small stockpot, over medium heat, heat the olive oil. Add onion; sauté until translucent. Add garlic; sauté until fragrant. Add turmeric, coriander, cinnamon, cumin, nutmeg, and chili powder; sauté until toasted and fragrant. Add stock; bring the mixture to a boil.

2. Add squash, zucchini, carrots, sweet potato, cauliflower, chickpeas, and raisins to a crockpot. Pour hot stock mixture over the vegetables.

3. Cook on high for 4-6 hours. Ladle the stew over couscous; garnish with parsley and sliced almonds.

Refried Bean
TACOS

PAREVE · YIELDS 10 SERVINGS

Growing up, we were never really bean eaters, aside from the occasional can of baked beans that my mom heated directly over the fire, right in the can. I didn't even know you could buy other canned beans until I was married. My husband, on the other hand, grew up on beans — from chickpeas to lima beans, his mom was always making stews. When I instituted Meatless Mondays in our home, beans were an obvious choice, and thankfully my kids take after my husband. This has become a family staple, and my kids request it again and again.

2 (15-oz.) cans	pinto beans
2 Tbsp	olive oil
1 small	onion, finely diced
2 cloves	garlic, minced
1 tsp	cumin
1 tsp	chili powder
¾ cup	vegetable stock
•	juice of ½ lime
•	salt, to taste
•	pepper, to taste
10	soft corn tortillas
1	avocado, peeled and thinly sliced
2	plum tomatoes, diced
•	lettuce, thinly sliced
•	nondairy sour cream
•	salsa

1. Drain and rinse the beans in a colander.

2. Heat olive oil in a large skillet; add onion. Sauté until translucent. Add garlic; sauté until fragrant. Add cumin and chili powder; sauté until toasted and aromatic. Add beans and stock; bring to a simmer.

3. Cook for a few minutes to soften beans; mash with a potato masher until the beans are mostly smooth with some chunky pieces. Add lime juice; season to taste with salt and pepper. For a smoother puree, process mixture in a food processor fitted with the "S" blade or in a blender until desired consistency is reached.

4. To serve, heat tortillas in a dry skillet (for a crispier taco, grease the skillet, or, for charred edges, toast over an open flame); fill with refried beans, sliced avocado, tomatoes, lettuce, nondairy sour cream, and salsa.

NOTE

If you make the refried beans in advance and they start to dry out, just stir in a bit more stock to make them creamy again.

VARIATION

If you'd like to make the tacos dairy, place the corn tortilla into a skillet for a minute so that it's pliable but not toasted. Add refried beans; top with shredded cheese. Cover the skillet and cook until tortilla is toasted and cheese is melted. Top with dairy sour cream and additional toppings, as desired.

SERVING SUGGESTIONS

• *Make burritos by filling tortillas with rice, refried beans, and toppings of choice.*

• *Make a Mexican dip by layering refried beans, guacamole, salsa or pico de gallo, and sour cream.*

• *Use as a base for a taco pizza with cheese and vegetables of your choice.*

Broccoli BURGERS

PAREVE · YIELDS 8 BURGERS · FREEZER FRIENDLY

I love a good beef burger with a runny egg (thankfully, I live just down the block from Boeuf & Bun!) but veggie burgers are a nice alternative when you're looking for something a little lighter. This recipe works great with good old cheddar cheese, but the cashew cheddar sauce is a must for dairy-free eaters.

32 oz.	frozen broccoli florets
2	eggs
1 Tbsp	olive oil
¼ cup	nutritional yeast
½ cup	almond meal
1 Tbsp	minced onion flakes
1 Tbsp	minced garlic flakes
▪	salt, to taste
▪	pepper, to taste

BREADING

1 cup	flaxseed meal
1 tsp	smoked paprika
½ tsp	oregano
½ tsp	chili powder
½ tsp	garlic powder
¼ tsp	kosher salt

FOR SERVING

- burger buns
- tomato slices
- lettuce
- red onion, sliced
- Cashew "Cheddar" Sauce, below

— NOTES —

If you don't have flaxseed meal, you can process flaxseeds in the food processor until ground, or you may use breadcrumbs, cornflake crumbs, or panko crumbs.

For dairy, omit olive oil and use Parmesan cheese instead of nutritional yeast. You may use slices of cheddar cheese instead of the "cheddar" sauce.

1. Preheat oven to 400°F. Line a baking sheet with parchment paper; coat with nonstick cooking spray.

2. Bring a pot of salted water to a boil over medium heat; add broccoli. Simmer until tender, about 10 minutes. Drain well.

3. Place broccoli into a food processor fitted with the "S" blade; pulse until very finely chopped but not ground. Transfer broccoli to a large bowl; add eggs, olive oil, nutritional yeast, almond meal, onion flakes, garlic flakes, salt, and pepper.

4. In a shallow bowl, combine the breading ingredients.

5. Using a ½-cup measuring cup, form patties; dredge patties in the breading mixture, pressing down to coat on all sides. Place the patties on prepared baking sheet; spray with nonstick cooking spray. Bake for 20 minutes.

6. Divide the burgers between buns; top with tomato, lettuce, onion, and "cheddar" sauce.

CASHEW "CHEDDAR" SAUCE

1 cup	roasted, unsalted cashews
¼ cup	water
1 Tbsp	miso
3 Tbsp	nutritional yeast
¼ tsp	smoked paprika
▪	juice of 1 lemon
½ tsp	kosher salt

- Add all sauce ingredients to a blender or a food processor fitted with the "S" blade; blend until smooth. Adjust consistency by adding more water, if desired.

Quinoa
PAD THAI BOWLS

PAREVE • YIELDS 4 SERVINGS

Pad Thai is a popular street food in Thailand, and it's the one I order at Asian restaurants. Traditionally, Pad Thai is made with rice noodles, but I used quinoa to up the protein content.

1½ cups	white quinoa
3 Tbsp	soy sauce
5 Tbsp	brown sugar
3 Tbsp	fresh-squeezed lime juice
1-2 Tbsp	sambal oelek OR chili garlic paste, to taste
2 tsp	toasted sesame oil
2 cloves	garlic, minced
1	carrot, julienned
3 cups	thinly sliced Napa cabbage
2 cups	bean sprouts
2	scallions, chopped
½ cup	roasted salted peanuts, chopped
•	handful cilantro
4	eggs

1. Place quinoa into a medium saucepan; add 2½ cups water. Bring to a boil; reduce heat, cover, and simmer for 10 minutes. Cool for 10 minutes; fluff with a fork. Set aside.

2. In a small bowl, combine soy sauce, brown sugar, lime juice and sambal oelek. Set aside.

3. In a wok or deep skillet, heat sesame oil over medium heat. Add garlic; sauté until fragrant, about 2 minutes. Add carrot and cabbage; sauté until tender, 3 minutes. Add sprouts; sauté for 1 minute.

4. Add quinoa and soy sauce mixture; stir to combine.

5. Divide Pad Thai between 4 bowls; garnish with scallions, peanuts, and cilantro.

6. Heat a nonstick frying pan over medium heat; coat with nonstick cooking spray. Add eggs, working in batches if necessary; cook sunny-side-up until the whites are set and the yolk is runny, about 3 minutes. Place an egg onto each quinoa bowl; serve immediately.

NOTES

If you can't find sambal oelek or chili garlic paste, you may use sriracha, to taste, instead.

Check the quinoa package to see if it should be rinsed before cooking; some brands are prewashed.

Vegetarian CHILI

PAREVE ▪ YIELDS 6 SERVINGS ▪ FREEZER FRIENDLY

As a food blogger, one of the things that give me the most nachas is getting photos of my recipes from my fans. When I created this recipe for my blog back in 2014, I wanted to create a dish that was hearty enough for meat eaters, yet still family friendly. I used this chili as a base for "chili pie in jars" which I filled with chili, cheddar cheese, and my World's Best Corn Muffin batter (page 46). The jars are baked in the oven for a super-fun dinner that kids just love. When the recipe went live, photos started pouring in of families sitting around the table with their Mason jars filled with chili and cornbread. I can't even describe the pride I felt in those moments, and that's what drives me to continue blogging to this very day.

1	onion, diced
3 cloves	garlic, minced
1½ Tbsp	olive oil
1	jalapeño, finely chopped (seeds and veins removed)
2 tsp	chili powder
½ tsp	cumin
1 tsp	garlic powder
3 heaping Tbsp	tomato paste
3	soft plum tomatoes, chopped small
2 Tbsp	brown sugar
1 (15-oz.) can	kidney beans, drained and rinsed
1 (15-oz.) can	pinto or black beans, drained and rinsed
2 cups	vegetable stock or water
▪	salt, to taste
▪	pepper, to taste

OPTIONAL TOPPINGS

- sliced avocado, corn kernels, shredded lettuce, diced tomatoes, crushed corn chips, salsa.
- For dairy meals, you can add sour cream and/or shredded cheddar cheese.

1. Heat olive oil in a pan over medium heat; add onions and garlic. Sauté until translucent. Add the jalapeño (add some of the veins and/or seeds for more heat); sauté for another minute. Add chili powder, cumin, and garlic; sauté until fragrant. Add tomato paste; sauté for 1-2 minutes.

2. Add remaining ingredients; bring to a simmer. Cook, covered, for 1 hour, stirring occasionally so that the chili doesn't stick to the bottom of the pan. Add additional stock, if desired, to reach desired consistency.

SERVING SUGGESTIONS

- *Serve with World's Best Corn Muffins (page 46) or make Chili Pie: Layer chili, cheddar cheese, and cornbread batter (mixed with scallions) into a dish. Bake until cornbread is cooked through.*

- *Make nachos by layering chili and cheddar cheese over tortilla chips; bake until cheese melts. Top with guacamole and salsa or toppings of choice.*

- *Serve over hot dogs, French fries, or baked potatoes with toppings of choice.*

- *Use as a base for Shepherd's Pie.*

DAIRY

No-Bake Stovetop Lasagna

Baklava Blintz Bundles

Nish Nosh Mac 'n Cheese

Spanakopita Quinoa Patties

Roasted Veggie & Goat Cheese Calzone Buns

Israeli Couscous Arancini

Beet Arugula Pizza with Pesto & Mozzarella

Cauliflower Poutine

No-Bake Stovetop
LASAGNA

DAIRY • YIELDS 8 SERVINGS

Shavuos — the holiday of cheesecake and lasagna — is the most anticipated of all holidays, but logistically it can get complicated. Because we have both meat and dairy meals, I keep the meat oven on and the stovetop off, and the dairy oven off, but the stovetop on. I prep my baked goods before the chag and leave the rest of the cooking for stovetop-only recipes. Of course, no one wants to forgo the cheesy lasagna, so I came up with this version that has become even more beloved than the original.

1 lb.	lasagna noodles
2 Tbsp	olive oil
3 cloves	garlic, minced
10 oz.	frozen chopped spinach, thawed, (1½ cups squeezed dry)
•	salt, to taste
•	pepper, to taste
1 (28-oz.) jar	marinara sauce
½ tsp	oregano
½ tsp	basil
8 oz.	ricotta cheese
2 cups	shredded mozzarella cheese

1. Fill a stock pot ¾-full with water; bring to a boil. Season generously with salt. Using your hands, break lasagna noodles into pieces; add them the water. Cook until pasta is tender, 8-10 minutes. Drain.

2. Heat olive oil in a deep skillet. Add garlic; sauté until fragrant. Add spinach; season, to taste, with salt and pepper. Add marinara sauce, oregano, and basil; bring to a simmer.

3. Add lasagna noodles, ricotta, and mozzarella; cook until cheeses have melted. Serve immediately.

Baklava
BLINTZ BUNDLES

DAIRY • YIELDS 24 BLINTZ BUNDLES • FREEZER FRIENDLY

Oh, blintzes, with your creamy (i.e., runny) cheese filling and your delicate (i.e., impossible to master until your batter is almost gone) crepe, you give me a run for my money. I was determined to come up with a fun twist on blintzes that did not involve standing over the stove ladling batter into the frying pan and swirling it just so, and let me just say, it was not an easy feat. My kids tried so many blintz variations until I made this one, and my pickiest kid looked up at me with his big blue eyes and said, "Ma, this is best thing you've ever made!" Success!

1 lb.	farmer cheese
8 oz.	block cream cheese (not whipped)
⅓ cup	sugar
2 tsp	lemon juice
½ tsp	vanilla extract
1	egg yolk
5 oz.	walnuts (1 cup chopped)
½ cup	brown sugar
½ tsp	cinnamon
¼ tsp	kosher salt
1 (16-oz.) pkg.	phyllo dough, thawed
1 stick	butter, melted

NOTE

The bundles may be made up to two days ahead. Reheat to crisp up before serving.

FREEZING INSTRUCTIONS

Freeze unbaked; bake frozen.

VARIATION

Instead of bundles, you can make traditional baklava by layering the phyllo sheets in a baking dish with the cheese and nut mixtures between each set of 4 layers. Bake until golden brown.

1. Line 2 baking sheets with parchment paper. Preheat oven to 375°F.

2. In a bowl, combine farmer cheese, cream cheese, sugar, lemon juice, vanilla, and egg yolk.

3. Add walnuts, brown sugar, cinnamon, and salt to a food processor or blender; pulse to lightly grind. (I prefer the nut mixture to have a finer grind, if you don't mind larger pieces of nuts, you may do this step by hand).

4. Lay a sheet of parchment paper on your work surface. Spread 1 sheet of phyllo dough onto the paper; brush lightly with melted butter. Top with a second sheet of phyllo dough. Repeat and top with two more sheets of phyllo, until you have a stack of four sheets. (Do not brush the top layer.) Cut the phyllo stack into 6 squares. Cover remaining phyllo sheets with a damp paper towel so they don't dry out while you fill the first bundles.

5. Place 1 heaping tablespoon of the cheese mixture in the center of a phyllo square. Top with 1 tablespoon of the nut mixture. Gather the phyllo dough over the filling to form a bundle. Place on prepared baking sheet.

6. Repeat with remaining squares, cheese, and nut mixture.

7. Repeat Steps 2-6 with remaining phyllo sheets until all the filling has been used.

8. Bake until browned and crisp, about 20 minutes. Remove the bundles to a wire rack to cool.

Nish Nosh
MAC 'N CHEESE

DAIRY ▪ YIELDS 8 SERVINGS

Nish Nosh crackers became popular a few years back with the famous Nish Nosh salad that made rounds around the world. The salad itself used only a handful of the crackers, and then you'd nibble on the rest of the bag because they were just so addictive. One week, when I was making mac 'n cheese, I was out of breadcrumbs, so I crushed some leftover crackers for the topping — and the rest is history.

1 (1-lb.) box	elbow pasta, prepared according to package directions
1 cup	sour cream
1 cup	whole milk
1	egg
1 tsp	onion powder
▪	salt, to taste
▪	pepper, to taste
8 oz.	shredded cheddar cheese
8 oz.	shredded mozzarella cheese
2 cups	Nish Nosh sour cream and onion crackers, crushed into crumbs
2 Tbsp	melted butter

1. Preheat oven to 375°F. Coat a casserole dish with butter or nonstick cooking spray.

2. In a large bowl, combine pasta, sour cream, milk, egg, onion powder, salt, pepper, and cheeses. Pour the mixture into prepared casserole dish. Sprinkle cracker crumbs over pasta mixture; drizzle with melted butter.

3. Bake until lightly golden, 20-25 minutes.

— NOTE —

Nish Nosh crackers are imported from Israel and are widely available in most kosher supermarkets, labeled Cracker Crisps, Sour Cream & Onion. If you can't find Nish Nosh Crackers, use crushed sour cream and onion potato chips.

Spanakopita
QUINOA PATTIES

DAIRY • YIELDS APPROXIMATELY 15 PATTIES • FREEZER FRIENDLY

Spanakopita, popular in Greek culture, is a spinach and feta pie made with phyllo dough. This quinoa version combines the classic pairing with the healthy grain, for crispy fried patties that can be served as an appetizer, or on a bun for a meatless meal.

1 Tbsp	olive oil
2 cloves	garlic, minced
1	shallot, minced
10 oz.	chopped frozen spinach (1½ cups squeezed dry)
▪	salt, to taste
▪	pepper, to taste
1 cup	uncooked quinoa, prepared according to package directions
1 cup	crumbled feta cheese
2	eggs + 1 egg white
▪	canola oil, for frying

1. Heat olive oil in a skillet over medium heat; add garlic and shallot. Sauté until fragrant. Add the spinach, season with salt and pepper, and sauté until heated through.

2. Place the prepared quinoa into a large mixing bowl. Add spinach mixture, feta, eggs, egg white, salt, and pepper.

3. Using a ¼-cup measuring cup, divide the mixture into patties. Heat canola oil in a skillet; fry the patties until golden brown on each side. Do not flip until a crust has fully formed on the patties.

― NOTE ―

The patties freeze well. Reheat frozen fried patties at 400°F until crispy.

Roasted Veggie & Goat Cheese
CALZONE BUNS

DAIRY · YIELDS 10 BUNS · FREEZER FRIENDLY

Cheesy pull-apart breads are a popular trend and this sophisticated spin on a vegetable calzone takes it from an everyday dish to a recipe worthy of special occasions.

10 oz.	cremini or button mushrooms, quartered
1 medium or 2 small	zucchini, cut into chunks
1	red onion, cut into chunks
3 Tbsp	olive oil, divided
½ tsp	dried basil
½ tsp	dried oregano
·	salt, to taste
·	pepper, to taste
2	red bell peppers
1 lb.	pizza dough
7 oz.	goat cheese
2 cups	shredded mozzarella cheese

ROASTED RED PEPPER DIP

2	roasted peppers; see Step 2
1 clove	garlic
¼ cup	light olive oil
2 tsp	fresh-squeezed lemon juice
½ tsp	balsamic vinegar
·	salt, to taste
·	pepper, to taste

— NOTE —

You may use feta or ricotta cheese instead of the goat cheese and substitute your choice of vegetables.

1. Preheat oven to 450°F. Line a deep pie dish with parchment paper. Grease the outside of a ramekin with cooking spray and place in the center of the dish.

2. On a baking sheet, toss mushrooms, zucchini, and onion with 2 tablespoons olive oil, basil, oregano, salt, and pepper. Move vegetables to one side of the baking sheet. Cut the red peppers in half; remove ribs and seeds. Place flesh-side down on the other side of the baking sheet; drizzle with remaining olive oil, salt and pepper. Roast for 45 minutes, stirring the vegetables (but not the peppers) occasionally. Remove peppers from the pan; wrap in foil. Set aside to use in Step 5.

3. Lower oven temperature to 375°F.

4. On a lightly floured surface, roll the pizza dough into a rectangle. Spread goat cheese over the dough, leaving a 1-inch border all around. Top with roasted vegetables and mozzarella. Starting from the longer side, roll the dough tightly into a log. Cut the dough into 10 slices; place into prepared pie dish, surrounding the ramekin. Bake for 45 minutes, or until the buns are puffed and starting to brown.

5. **Prepare the roasted red pepper dip:** Take reserved peppers out of the foil; peel off the skins. Place the roasted peppers into a food processor or blender; add remaining dip ingredients. Blend until smooth. Pour into prepared ramekin before serving.

Israeli Couscous
ARANCINI

DAIRY • YIELDS 12 SERVINGS • FREEZER FRIENDLY

Arancini is one of my favorite dairy indulgences. Originally from Italy, they are deep-fried risotto balls stuffed with cheese — mozzarella sticks on steroids. Making arancini from scratch can be a lengthy process, since it starts with risotto, so I simplified the dish by using Israeli couscous. These deep-fried squares of cheesy goodness make a super-fun party appetizer that kids love!

1 Tbsp	butter
¼ cup	minced shallots (from 2 small)
2 cloves	garlic, minced
1 (8.8-oz.) bag	Israeli couscous
2 cups	whole milk
½ tsp	kosher salt
2 cups	shredded mozzarella
3	eggs
•	salt, to taste
•	pepper, to taste
2 cups	panko crumbs
1 tsp	dried basil
1 tsp	dried oregano
½ tsp	garlic powder
•	canola oil, for frying
•	grated Parmesan cheese, for dusting
•	marinara sauce, for serving

1. In a large saucepan, over medium heat, melt butter. Add shallot and garlic; sauté until softened and fragrant. Add couscous, milk, and salt; bring the mixture to a simmer.

2. Cook until couscous is tender and milk is absorbed (watch carefully, as it can boil over easily), about 8 minutes. Stir in the mozzarella.

3. Pour couscous mixture into a 9x9-inch pan; refrigerate until pasta is solid, about 1 hour. Remove from the pan and cut into 1½ x 1½-inch cubes.

4. In a shallow bowl, beat eggs lightly; season with salt and pepper.

5. In a second shallow bowl, combine panko crumbs, basil, oregano, and garlic powder. Mix to combine; season with salt and pepper.

6. Heat 2 inches of canola oil in a deep skillet over medium-high heat. Working in batches, dip the pasta cubes first in eggs and then in panko crumb mixture, to coat. Fry until golden and drain on paper towels.

7. Dust the arancini with Parmesan; serve with marinara sauce, for dipping.

--- NOTE ---

To prepare in advance, you may freeze the arancini before or after frying. You may fry unfried frozen arancini until browned and crisp. If arancini have already been fried, bake at 400°F on a greased baking sheet until crispy and heated through.

Beet Arugula Pizza
WITH PESTO & MOZZARELLA

DAIRY ▪ YIELDS 8 SERVINGS

I'm not into making classic homemade pizza, because honestly, I really like the stuff I can get in the pizza store. Living in Brooklyn, there's a plethora of pizza shops, each with its devoutly loyal customer base (I'm partial to Pizza Time in Flatbush!). If I'm going to make homemade pizza, it's got to be something I can't get in the store. It's got to be made with fresh ingredients and top quality cheese — and the flavors had better pop. This right here is homemade pizza that is worth making. Even if you live in Brooklyn.

1 lb.	pizza dough
1 tsp	cornmeal
⅔ cup	Spinach Pistachio Pesto *(page 36)*
1 small	beet, thinly sliced
8 ounces	fresh mozzarella, thinly sliced
1 Tbsp	olive oil
1 cup	arugula, lightly packed

— NOTE —

If desired, lightly dress the arugula with olive oil, lemon juice, salt, and pepper.

1. Place a pizza stone or baking sheet into a cold oven; set the oven temperature to 450°F. Allow to preheat for 20 minutes while you prepare the pizza. Coat a sheet of parchment paper with nonstick cooking spray; sprinkle with cornmeal.

2. Roll out the dough into desired shape; place on prepared parchment paper.

3. Spread pesto over dough; top with beets and mozzarella. Drizzle oil over the pizza.

4. Lower oven temperature to 400°F.

5. Slide out the oven rack so you can transfer the pizza. Lifting the parchment paper by the sides; transfer it to the heated pizza stone or baking sheet.

6. Bake for 20-25 minutes or until the dough is browned and crispy.

7. Top with arugula before serving.

Cauliflower
POUTINE

DAIRY · YIELDS 6 SERVINGS

My first taste of poutine was at Pita Pizza in Montreal. I had never heard of the dish before, but everyone around me seemed to be ordering it, so I gave it a try. Oh. Em. Gee. It took comfort food to the next level. Poutine is the national dish of Quebec and it involves creamy gravy-smothered french fries with lots of gooey melted cheese. When I got home, I was determined to recreate the dish and came up with the idea of a poutine latke. The Canadians went wild, posting it on many popular websites, and I ended up cooking the dish for an article that was featured in The Wall Street Journal. I even made the front page! After turning classic poutine into an even more indulgent dish, I thought it was time to lighten up the classic, so I came up with this cauliflower version, to be enjoyed without the guilt.

2 heads	cauliflower, cut into florets
2 Tbsp	olive oil
▪	salt, to taste
▪	pepper, to taste

POUTINE GRAVY

2 Tbsp	butter
2 cloves	garlic, minced
3 Tbsp	flour
2 cups	vegetable stock
1 Tbsp	soy sauce
¼ cup	grated Parmesan cheese
▪	salt, to taste
▪	pepper, to taste
8 oz.	shredded mozzarella cheese

1. Preheat oven to 425°F. Spread the cauliflower on a baking sheet. Drizzle with oil; season with salt and pepper. Bake until tender and crisped, about 30 minutes. Remove from oven; do not turn off heat.

2. **Meanwhile, prepare the poutine gravy:** Add butter to a saucepan; melt over medium heat. Add garlic; stir until softened and fragrant, but not browned. Add flour; stir to form a paste. Continue stirring over medium heat until golden. Slowly add stock, whisking as you pour. Raise heat; continue to whisk until mixture comes to a boil.

3. Reduce heat to a simmer. Add soy sauce and Parmesan, whisking until mixture is smooth and thickened. Season, to taste, with salt and pepper.

4. Pour gravy over cauliflower; top with mozzarella and return to the oven. Bake until cheese is melted and bubbly, about 5 minutes.

— VARIATION —

You may also use frozen breaded cauliflower in place of the roasted cauliflower. Cook according to package directions and proceed as above.

SIDES

Sugar-Free Butternut Squash Pie

Honey Harissa Roasted Cauliflower

Roasted Tricolor Beets with Grapefruit Gremolata

Parsnip Puree

Confetti Cabbage

Everyday Roasted Veggies

Garlic Green Beans with Roasted Tomatoes

Herbed Potato Wedges

Lokshin & Cabbage with Apples & Honey

Roasted Sweet Potatoes with Gooey Pecans

Sugar-Free BUTTERNUT SQUASH PIE

PAREVE ▪ YIELDS 1 (9-INCH) PIE ▪ FREEZER FRIENDLY

A couple of years back, I did a few rounds of the Whole30 diet — a 30-day nutrition reset that is based on the Paleo diet. The cleanse is severely restrictive, with no dairy, soy, legumes, sugar (or sugar substitutes), or grains allowed. I came up with lots of nutritious and satisfying meals, notwithstanding the restrictions, and I decided to sell a 30-Day Meal Plan on my blog for others to enjoy. I never imagined I would sell thousands of copies, but the feedback was incredibly satisfying, and the plan helped so many people lose weight without feeling deprived. This butternut squash pie is the dish I make the most from the plan because I managed to recreate a family favorite with no added sweetener. The trick is roasting the squash to concentrate its natural sweetness, and as a bonus, no peeling is required.

1 (2.5-lb.)	butternut squash
1 cup	full-fat canned coconut milk
2 Tbsp	coconut oil, melted
2	eggs
½ tsp	cinnamon, plus more for topping
¼ tsp	kosher salt

NOTE

For an extra creamy pie, puree mixture with a hand blender before adding to pie dish. If you prefer added sweetener, add a bit of maple syrup, to taste.

1. Preheat oven to 400°F. Line a baking sheet with parchment paper; coat with non stick cooking spray.

2. Cut butternut squash in half lengthwise; remove seeds. Place on baking sheet, cut side down; bake until roasted and caramelized, about one hour (peel should be browned in spots).

3. Scoop the flesh from the squash into a bowl. Combine with coconut milk, coconut oil, eggs, cinnamon, and salt.

4. Lower oven temperature to 350°F. Coat a 9-inch pie dish with nonstick cooking spray.

5. Place mixture into prepared pie dish; sprinkle with additional cinnamon. Bake until set, about 45 minutes.

Honey Harissa
ROASTED CAULIFLOWER

PAREVE ▪ YIELDS 4-6 SERVINGS

Balance is an important part of cooking and contrasting sweet and spicy flavors is my jam. Honey and harissa are a perfect pairing, and they turn healthy cauliflower into a must-have dish.

2 Tbsp	olive oil
2 Tbsp	honey
1 Tbsp	harissa
1 head	cauliflower, cut into florets
▪	salt, to taste

1. Preheat oven to 450°F.

2. In a large bowl, combine olive oil, honey, and harissa. Add cauliflower; toss to coat. Spread the cauliflower in a single layer on a baking sheet; season with salt.

3. Roast on the lower rack for 25-30 minutes, tossing once, or until tender and starting to crisp up around the edges.

Roasted Tricolor Beets
WITH GRAPEFRUIT GREMOLATA

PAREVE ▪ YIELDS 10 SERVINGS

When I was growing up, we ate beets only once a year — on Pesach. My mother would boil them with potatoes and carrots for her traditional Vinaigrette Salad. After I was married, I was surprised to see beets, or as my Spanish-speaking in-laws called them, "remolacha," on the table each and every Shabbos. I took a liking to them and was happy to learn that they also come in both golden yellow and candy-striped colors (which turn pink when roasted). Beets are inherently sweet, especially so when roasted, and this simple preparation really allows them to shine.

2 medium   red beets
2 medium   golden beets
2 medium   Chioggia (a.k.a. Candy Cane) beets

GREMOLATA

1 cup   loosely packed parsley, finely chopped
2 Tbsp   grapefruit zest (from 1 grapefruit)
1 Tbsp   freshly-squeezed grapefruit juice
1 clove   garlic, minced
2 Tbsp   olive oil
▪   salt, to taste
▪   pepper, to taste
▪   Maldon sea salt flakes, for finishing, optional

1. Preheat oven to 400°F.

2. Wash the beets well; wrap each beet individually in foil. Place on a baking sheet; bake until tender when pierced with a fork, about 1 hour. Remove from the oven; cool completely (do not unwrap).

3. When the beets have cooled, open the foil packets and pull the peels off the beets; they will slide right off. (This works well with red and golden beets, you may need to peel Chioggia with a knife.)

4. Cut the beets into ¼-inch slices; arrange on a platter, overlapping slightly.

5. **Prepare the gremolata:** In a bowl, toss together parsley, grapefruit zest, grapefruit juice, garlic, olive oil, salt, and pepper.

6. Drizzle gremolata over beets; top with Maldon flakes, if desired.

NOTE

Traditionally, gremolata is meant as a garnish or condiment. If you want to use it as more of a dressing, you can add a bit more olive oil or double the recipe.

VARIATION

*You may use lemon or orange zest and juice instead of the grapefruit, or use mint instead of parsley.
Top with chopped nuts or dukkah (a nut and seed blend).*

Parsnip PUREE

PAREVE ▪ YIELDS 6 SERVINGS ▪ FREEZER FRIENDLY

Parsnip puree is the Millennial mashed potato — lighter, silkier, and infinitely more sophisticated. The best part is, there are no tricks to the "creamiest mashed parsnips" — the root vegetable puree is silky smooth in its own right. Its sweet and nutty flavor pairs well with most proteins, especially duck, lamb, and beef.

2 lbs.	parsnips, peeled and roughly chopped
▪	salt, to taste
2 Tbsp	coconut oil
¼ cup	coconut milk, any variety
⅛ tsp	nutmeg

1. Add parsnips to a medium saucepan; cover with water. Season with salt. Bring to a boil, reduce to a simmer, and cook for about 15 minutes, until the parsnips are soft and tender. Drain.

2. Place parsnips into a food processor fitted with the "S" blade or to a blender; add remaining ingredients. Blend until smooth and creamy.

— NOTE —

The coconut flavor takes a back seat to the rich flavor of parsnip in this puree and is virtually undetectable; however, if you prefer not to use coconut products, you may use vegan butter or oil in place of the coconut oil, and non-dairy milk or stock in place of the coconut milk.

Confetti CABBAGE

PAREVE · YIELDS 4-6 SERVINGS

This one goes out to my favorite foodie and good friend Mel of @kitchentested. Mel got me, and lots of other foodie followers, into roasted red cabbage steaks. I never imagined roasted cabbage could be so delicious, so I came up with a confetti version with both green and red cabbage combined. I like to spice it with Montreal steak seasoning for a crunchy and salty bite, but you can use any spice you choose. It's important to use fresh cabbage here, so don't buy the prepackaged version.

½ small	red cabbage, sliced into ⅓-inch strips
½ small	green cabbage, sliced into ⅓-inch strips
2 Tbsp	olive oil
1 Tbsp	Montreal steak seasoning

1. Preheat oven to 425°F. Spread cabbage in a single layer on 2 baking sheets; drizzle with olive oil. Season with Montreal steak seasoning; stir until evenly coated.

2. Roast for 20 minutes, stirring once, until the cabbage is tender and starting to brown.

Everyday
ROASTED VEGGIES

PAREVE ▪ YIELDS 4-6 SERVINGS

Roasted veggies are a staple in my house because there always seems to be some extra vegetables around that I need to use up. Roasting breathes new life into produce that is slightly past its prime, so don't ever waste — just roast, roast, roast. You can enjoy roasted veggies on their own, or add them to salads, grain bowls, wraps and sandwiches.

1 small	zucchini, sliced on a bias
1 small	eggplant, sliced on a bias
1	red onion, cut into wedges
10-oz.	mushrooms, halved
2 Tbsp	olive oil
1 Tbsp	balsamic vinegar
1 tsp	oregano
▪	salt, to taste
▪	pepper, to taste

1. Preheat oven to 450°F. Place vegetables on a baking sheet; drizzle with oil and vinegar. Season with oregano, salt, and pepper; stir to coat vegetables.

2. Roast for about 30 minutes, stirring occasionally, until vegetables are tender and lightly caramelized.

Garlic Green Beans
WITH ROASTED TOMATOES

PAREVE ▪ YIELDS: 6-8 SERVINGS

This recipe happened as a means of presentation, more than anything. I'm always thinking about how I can add color to a dish, so one Shabbat, I topped my roasted asparagus with my basic fridge stock: fire-roasted grape tomatoes. The dish was so beautiful that I continued to make it, using snap peas and green beans, too.

1 lb.	green beans, ends trimmed
2 Tbsp	olive oil
3 cloves	garlic, minced
▪	zest of 1 lemon
▪	salt, to taste
▪	pepper, to taste
1 cup	Fire-Roasted Grape Tomatoes (page 28)
2 Tbsp	pine nuts

1. Preheat oven to 400°F. Line a baking sheet with parchment paper.

2. Spread green beans out on prepared baking sheet; toss with olive oil, garlic, lemon zest, salt, and pepper.

3. Bake for about 25 minutes, stirring once, until tender-crisp. While the green beans are baking, place the pine nuts into a small baking dish and toast in the oven for 5 minutes, or until lightly browned. Chop roughly if desired.

4. Spread the green beans out on a serving tray; top with roasted tomatoes and pine nuts. Serve warm.

— NOTE —

If you don't have prepared fire roasted tomatoes, you may roast the tomatoes on a separate pan in the oven while you are roasting the green beans. Follow the recipe on page 28, roasting them at 400°F instead of broiling, until browned, about 25 minutes.

— VARIATION —

You may also use other nuts, such as hazelnuts, macadamia nuts, pistachios, or almonds.

Herbed
POTATO WEDGES

PAREVE ▪ YIELDS 6 SERVINGS

Ah, french fries, who doesn't love them? These herbed potato wedges are my homemade answer to french fries. The peel offers some added fiber and the fresh herbs make me feel like I'm eating something a bit more green. Easy homemade dips are essential, so I always have truffle mayo and sriracha ketchup on hand.

5 large	russet (Idaho) potatoes
¼ cup	lightly packed chopped parsley
¼ cup	lightly packed chopped cilantro
4 cloves	garlic, minced
1½ tsp	cumin
2 tsp	kosher salt
¼ tsp	pepper
¼ cup	olive oil

— NOTE —

Truffle oils vary in the strength of their truffle flavor. Adjust according to your taste.

1. Preheat oven to 425°F. Line 2 baking sheets with parchment paper.

2. Scrub the potatoes well. Cut in half lengthwise; cut each half into quarters. Cut each quarter into 2-3 wedges (depending on size of potatoes).

3. Combine remaining ingredients in a large bowl. Add potato wedges; stir to coat potatoes with spices and oil. Divide wedges between prepared baking sheets.

4. Bake for 25 minutes, turn wedges over, and rotate pans. Bake for an additional 20-25 minutes, until browned and crispy.

5. Serve with Truffle Mayonnaise and/or Sriracha Ketchup.

TRUFFLE MAYONNAISE

½ cup	mayonnaise
2 tsp	white truffle oil
1 tsp	Dijon mustard
▪	salt, to taste
▪	coarsely ground black pepper, to taste

- In a small bowl, stir ingredients together.

SRIRACHA KETCHUP

½ cup	ketchup
4 tsp	sriracha
2 Tbsp	honey
2 tsp	freshly squeezed lime juice
½ tsp	smoked paprika

- In a small bowl, stir ingredients together.

Lokshin & Cabbage
WITH APPLES & HONEY

PAREVE ▪ YIELDS 6 SERVINGS

Lokshin and cabbage is a classic Ashkenazi dish that I grew up eating. My mom always made it extra sweet, with a heavy dose of sugar and lots of love. It was usually served over the holidays, so I decided to turn the classic into a festive Rosh Hashanah dish by adding these symbolic foods: leeks, apples, and honey.

¼ cup	light olive oil, divided
1 large	leek, sliced
2	Fuji apples, peeled and diced small
10 oz.	shredded cabbage
▪	salt, to taste
▪	pepper, to taste
¼ cup	honey
10 oz.	wide egg noodles, prepared according to package directions

1. Heat 2 tablespoons oil in a deep skillet; add the leek. Sauté over medium heat until leek is wilted and starting to brown, about 5 minutes. Add apples; sauté until softened.

2. Add cabbage, salt, and pepper; cook over medium heat, stirring occasionally, until wilted and starting to caramelize, about 10 minutes. Remove from heat.

3. Add honey, remaining 2 tablespoons oil, and noodles; stir to incorporate. Season with additional salt and pepper.

Roasted Sweet Potatoes
WITH GOOEY PECANS

MEAT • YIELDS 6 SERVINGS

Baked sweet potatoes sound easy enough — you buy some sweet potatoes, wrap them in foil, and bake until soft, right? Wrong. First off, if you've never tried organic sweet potatoes, you don't know what you're missing. I don't usually push the organic envelope, but when it comes to sweet potatoes, it's everything. Where traditional sweet potatoes are often stringy and watery, organic sweet potatoes are intensely rich and almost fudgy. I bake them uncovered until soft, and trust me when I tell you — they're going to change your sweet potato game.

6	sweet potatoes, organic preferred
8 oz.	beef fry, chopped
1 cup	chopped roasted pecans
½ cup	pure maple syrup (NOT pancake syrup)
½ cup	brown sugar
•	salt, to taste
•	pepper, to taste

— NOTE —

If the filling solidifies before serving, warm gently over low heat before serving.

1. Preheat oven to 425°F.

2. Wash sweet potatoes well; place into a baking dish. Bake, uncovered, turning once, until soft, 50-60 minutes, depending on the size of sweet potatoes.

3. In a skillet, fry the beef fry until crispy; remove from the pan, reserving the fat. Drain on paper towels.

4. To the same skillet, add pecans, maple syrup, brown sugar, salt, and pepper; bring the mixture to a simmer. Cook until mixture thickens, about 1 minute. Remove from heat; cool slightly (it will thicken more as it cools). Stir in the crisped beef fry.

5. Make a slit in each sweet potato; stuff with gooey pecans. Serve warm.

CAKES, PIES, & TARTS

Mile High S'mores Pie

Seasonal Fruit Crisp Winter

Seasonal Fruit Crisp Summer

Frangipane Fig Galette

Mason Jar Honey Cakes

Orange Creamsicle Cheesecake

Chocolate Hazelnut Ganache Tart with Macaroon Crust

Red Wine Chocolate Cake with Poached Pears

Mile High S'MORES PIE

PAREVE ▪ YIELDS 10 SERVINGS ▪ FREEZER FRIENDLY

You know how families have a signature dessert that they make for birthdays, parties, and other get-togethers? Well, this is ours. I developed this recipe a few years back, when just a short time before Shabbos, I had some unexpected guests and I realized I hadn't made any dessert. I grabbed whatever I could find in the pantry, and the Mile High S'mores Pie was born. My kids request it again and again, and they never get bored of the crunchy marshmallow goodness.

1 graham cracker pie crust

GANACHE

8 oz. good-quality regular size chocolate chips (1¼ cups regular size)

1 cup full-fat canned coconut milk

1 tsp vanilla extract

pinch sea salt

TOPPING

2 Tbsp coconut oil

16 oz. marshmallow fluff

8-10 cups cornflakes

1. **Prepare the ganache:** Pour chocolate chips into a medium heatproof bowl; set aside. Place the coconut milk into a small saucepan; bring to a simmer over medium heat. Pour hot milk over chocolate chips; let stand for a few minutes, until chocolate softens. Stir until smooth; add the vanilla and salt. Pour the ganache into the pie crust; place in freezer to set.

2. **Prepare the topping:** When ganache has set, melt coconut oil in a large saucepan; add marshmallow fluff. Stir until melted. Add the cornflakes; stir to coat evenly.

3. Remove pie from the freezer; top with cornflake mixture. Refrigerate until ready to serve.

Seasonal Fruit Crisp
WINTER

PAREVE ▪ YIELDS 10 SERVINGS ▪ FREEZER FRIENDLY

You'll often find fruit crisp served as a side dish for the Shabbos meal, but I think of it as more of a dessert, to be served with ice cream. I make different versions, depending on the season, but you can feel free to play around with your own combination of seasonal fruit. I love the combo of cranberry, apples and pears — it's tangy and sweet at the same time, and who doesn't love a traditional oatmeal crumble?

CRANBERRY APPLE & PEAR CRISP

2	pears, peeled and diced
4	apples, peeled and diced
12 oz.	fresh or frozen cranberries
½ cup	sugar
1½ Tbsp	cornstarch
1 tsp	cinnamon
2 tsp	fresh-squeezed lemon juice

OAT CRUMBLE

1 cup	flour
¾ cup	old-fashioned oats
⅔ cup	brown sugar
½ tsp	cinnamon
½ cup	melted coconut oil or any neutral-flavored oil
pinch	salt
▪	ice cream, for serving, optional

1. Preheat oven to 375°F. Place pears, apples, cranberries, sugar, cornstarch, cinnamon, and lemon juice into an oven-to-table baking dish; stir to incorporate.

2. Cover the dish with foil; bake until cranberries burst and start to release their juices, about 25 minutes.

3. Meanwhile, prepare the crumble topping: In a small bowl, combine flour, oats, brown sugar, cinnamon, oil, and salt. Stir until crumbly.

4. Sprinkle crumble over the fruit; lower the oven temperature to 350°F, return to the oven. Bake, uncovered for 20-25 minutes, until the fruit is bubbly and the topping is crisp. Serve warm with ice cream, if desired.

Seasonal Fruit Crisp
SUMMER

PAREVE • YIELDS 10 SERVINGS • FREEZER FRIENDLY

Ah marzipan - you either love it or hate it! In my house, we call anything with marzipan, rainbow-cookie-flavored because the three color cookies are my husband's nosh of choice. My kids are big fans too, so it's no wonder that I sneak it into my fruit crisp topping. The almond flavor pairs so well with summer berries, you'll want to make it for winter too — and I've got you covered with a frozen fruit variation!

BLUEBERRY CHERRY CRISP

3 cups	blueberries
3 cups	cherries, pitted and halved
2 Tbsp	cornstarch
1 Tbsp	lemon juice
½ cup	sugar

MARZIPAN CRUMBLE

1 cup	flour
⅓ cup	sugar
⅓ cup	neutral-flavored oil
1 tsp	almond extract
⅓ cup	sliced almonds
pinch	salt
4 oz.	marzipan, crumbled
½ tsp	cinnamon

1. Preheat oven to 350°F.

2. In an oven-to-table baking dish, combine blueberries, cherries, cornstarch, lemon juice, and sugar. Stir to incorporate.

3. Prepare the crumble topping: In a small bowl, combine flour, sugar, oil, almond extract, sliced almonds, salt, and marzipan.

4. Spread crumble over the fruit; sprinkle with cinnamon.

5. Bake, uncovered, for 45 minutes, or until the fruit is bubbly and the crumble is crisp.

— NOTE —

You may use 4 (12-oz.) packages of frozen blueberries, cherries, or other berries. Lightly thaw fruit and continue as above. For individual servings, divide the fruit and topping into ramekins; bake for 35-40 minutes.

Frangipane Fig GALETTE

DAIRY ▪ YIELDS 8 SERVINGS ▪ FREEZER FRIENDLY

I first learned of frangipane, an almond-scented pastry cream, at a pastry class at the Center for Kosher Culinary Arts. Frangipane is made from its more popular cousin, marzipan — an almond paste that gives many Pesach desserts their unique almond flavor.

1¼ cups	flour
½ cup (2 oz.)	slivered blanched almonds
¼ cup	sugar
¼ tsp	kosher salt
½ cup (1 stick)	butter, cut into pieces
½ tsp	almond extract
1-2 Tbsp	ice water
12 oz.	fresh figs OR other seasonal fruit, such as apples, pears, apricots, peaches, nectarines, or plums
1 egg + 1 Tbsp	water, for egg wash
1 Tbsp	demerara sugar
2 Tbsp	silan OR honey

FRANGIPANE FILLING

1 cup	slivered almonds
½ cup	sugar
½ cup (1 stick)	butter, cut into 1-inch slices
1 large	egg
3 Tbsp	flour
2 tsp	almond extract
⅛ tsp	kosher salt

— QUICK & EASY —

Use puff pastry sheets instead of the homemade crust. Unfold 1 sheet of pastry and place onto a parchment-lined baking sheet. Brush egg wash around the edge of the pastry and fold over to create a ½-inch border. Using a fork, prick the pastry all around, inside the border. Pipe half the frangipane filling into the tart and top with half of your fruit of choice. Repeat with remaining ingredients. Yields 2 puff pastry tarts.

1. **Prepare the dough:** Line a baking sheet with parchment paper.

2. Using a food processor fitted with the "S" blade, blend flour, almonds, sugar, and salt until nuts are finely ground. Add butter; pulse until mixture resembles coarse meal. Mix in almond extract and enough ice water to form moist clumps.

3. Turn mixture onto a work surface; pack the clumps together to form a disk. Wrap in plastic wrap; refrigerate until firm, 30 minutes.

4. **Meanwhile, prepare the frangipane filling:** Add almonds and sugar to the food processor (you don't need to clean it out); process until almonds are finely ground (the sugar keeps it from turning to almond butter). Add remaining frangipane ingredients; blend until smooth. Transfer mixture to a pastry bag or ziplock bag. Refrigerate while you prepare the pastry.

5. Preheat the oven to 375°F.

6. Remove the dough from the fridge; roll it out to a 13-14-inch circle. Place the dough onto prepared baking sheet. Snip off one corner of the ziplock bag, if using. Pipe the frangipane filling onto the dough, leaving a 2-inch border.

7. Remove and discard fig stems. Slice figs; layer slices over the frangipane, overlapping them slightly. Fold the dough over the filling, forming pleats all around, leaving the center open. Brush the dough with eggwash; sprinkle with demerara sugar.

8. Bake for 35 minutes, or until galette is golden and crispy.

9. Brush silan over the exposed figs.

Mason Jar
HONEY CAKES

PAREVE · YIELDS 5 JARS

Millennials have come to love Mason jars almost as much as they hate honey cake, but I'm determined to change that. This honey cake recipe has converted many a honey cake-hater and hails to us all the way from Melbourne, Australia. My sister received the recipe on a handout from her son's teacher, Mrs. Dina Lili Sziewicz, many years back. After sharing it on my blog back in 2013, it has become a holiday staple in Jewish homes around the world. This recipe isn't heavily spiced or dry, but simply sweet and remarkably fudgy. I bake the cakes right in the Mason jars and give them out to my kids' teachers before Rosh Hashanah to get the year off to a sweet start.

2	eggs
1 cup	sugar
½ cup	canola oil
1 cup	honey
1 cup	self-rising flour (see Tip)
1 cup	regular flour
1 Tbsp	cocoa
½ tsp	cinnamon
½ tsp	baking soda
1 cup	boiling water

SPECIAL EQUIPMENT

5   wide-mouth pint jars

1. Preheat oven to 350°F.

2. Beat eggs and sugar until creamy. Add oil and honey; beat until incorporated.

3. In a second bowl, mix flours, cocoa, cinnamon, and baking soda. Add dry ingredients to wet ingredients; beat until incorporated. Pour boiling water into the batter; mix with a spoon until creamy.

4. Wash jars with hot water (see Note) and dry well. Coat the inside of the jars with nonstick cooking spray.

5. Fill jars halfway with cake batter; place on a baking sheet. Bake for 25-30 minutes, or until a toothpick inserted into the center comes out clean. Cool completely on a rack or kitchen towel (do not place directly on the countertop; see Note); seal jars.

── NOTES ──

Mason jars are traditionally used for preserving and canning. Since they are not made of tempered glass, it's important not to expose them to drastic temperature changes, because they can burst. For that reason, I prefer to warm the glasses by washing in hot water and I cool them on a rack or dishtowel, but never on a cold counter.

Honey cakes can also be baked in mini loaf pans.

── TIP ──

If you don't have self-rising flour, add 1 tsp salt + 1½ tsp baking powder to a measuring cup; add flour to measure 1 cup.

Orange Creamsicle
CHEESECAKE

DAIRY • YIELDS 12-16 SERVINGS • FREEZER FRIENDLY

Some of my most cherished childhood memories were of summers spent in the bungalow colony in upstate New York. There are certain foods that take me back to the smell of the grass in Himmel's: Kool-Aid, Trix cereal, and creamsicle ice cream. The sweet vanilla and orange combination offered a refreshing reprieve from the summer heat, and I've recreated those flavors here, in the form of a cheesecake.

2 cups	graham cracker crumbs from about 1½ sleeves of crackers
6 Tbsp	butter, melted
1¼ cups	sugar, divided
3 (8-oz) pkgs	brick cream cheese, at room temperature
8 oz.	sour cream
3	eggs
1 Tbsp	vanilla extract
1 tsp	orange zest
1 Tbsp	freshly squeezed orange juice
3 drops	yellow food coloring
2 drops	red food coloring

1. Preheat oven to 350°F. Cut a circle of parchment paper to line the base of a 9-inch springform pan. Wrap the outside of the pan in a double layer of foil, covering the underside and extending up the sides of the pan.

2. In a small bowl, combine graham cracker crumbs, butter, and ¼ cup sugar. Press the mixture into prepared pan.

3. Using a hand mixer, beat cream cheese and remaining 1 cup sugar in large bowl until blended. Add sour cream and vanilla; mix well. Add eggs, 1 at a time, beating on low speed after each addition just until blended.

4. Transfer 2 cups of the batter to a medium bowl. Add orange zest, orange juice, and food coloring.

5. Reserve ½ cup plain batter. Pour remaining plain batter into the pan. Refrigerate for 15 minutes to set.

6. Top with a layer of the orange cheesecake batter. Drop spoonfuls of the remaining plain batter over the top of the orange batter; run a knife through it to create a marbled effect.

7. **Prepare a water bath:** Place the springform pan into a larger roasting pan, pull out the oven rack, and place the roasting pan on it. Pour boiling water into the roasting pan, taking care not to get any water in the cheesecake, until it reaches about halfway up the sides of the springform pan.

8. Bake for about 1 hour, or until the center jiggles slightly, but the rest of the cheesecake is set. Turn the oven off and leave the cheesecake in the oven for one hour, with the door slightly ajar.

9. Refrigerate overnight to set. Remove sides of the springform pan to serve.

Chocolate Hazelnut Ganache Tart
WITH MACAROON CRUST

PAREVE ▪ YIELDS 10-12 SERVINGS ▪ FREEZER FRIENDLY

Having my recipes featured on the back of food packaging was always on my blogger bucket list because it meant that I wasn't just a home cook who blogged in her spare time, but a serious recipe developer. I checked that off my list when California Gourmet printed my chocolate ganache tart with a macaroon crust on their bag of chocolate chips, and the Pesach-friendly dessert has been wowing audiences for years. I've taken the gluten-free tart to the next level with a homemade hazelnut ganache that is reminiscent of Nutella.

TART CRUST

7 oz.	sweetened coconut flakes or shredded coconut (2 cups)
9 oz.	Medjool dates, pitted (about 11 dates)

GANACHE

10 oz.	hazelnuts (2 cups)
8 oz.	chocolate chips (1¼ cups regular size)
1 cup	full-fat canned coconut milk
2 tsp	vanilla extract
▪	sea salt, to taste

OPTIONAL TOPPINGS

- Coconut Whipped Cream (page 286), toasted shredded coconut, fresh berries

— STORAGE —

This tart freezes beautifully. Thaw in the refrigerator for a few hours before serving.

1. Preheat oven to 350°F. Line a 9-inch tart pan with parchment paper so that it hangs over the sides.

2. **Prepare the crust:** Spread coconut flakes onto a baking sheet; bake for 10-12 minutes, stirring every few minutes, until golden brown. Set aside to cool for a few minutes.

3. Add dates and toasted coconut to a food processor fitted with the "S" blade; process until ingredients are well incorporated and they reach a dough-like consistency. If the dough is greasy (a result of blending the toasted coconut, which releases its natural oils), pat dry with a paper towel.

4. Press the dough into prepared tart pan, spreading it out and up the sides like a pie crust.

5. **Prepare the ganache:** Spread hazelnuts on a baking sheet; bake for 12-15 minutes, until nuts are fragrant and skins are starting to crack.

6. Wrap nuts in a clean kitchen towel; use your hands to roll nuts around in the towel to remove most of the skins. Then place the nuts into a food processor fitted with the "S" blade. Blend nuts until a nut butter forms; this can take 5-10 minutes depending on the quality of your machine; be patient! Scrape down the bowl of the processor every few minutes as the nuts go from ground, to pasty, and finally to creamy.

7. Add chocolate chips, coconut milk, vanilla, and sea salt to the food processor; blend until smooth.

8. Pour the ganache into the crust; refrigerate until firm.

9. Use the overhanging parchment paper to lift the tart out of the tart pan. Slice and serve.

Red Wine Chocolate Cake
WITH POACHED PEARS

PAREVE · YIELDS 12-15 SERVINGS · FREEZER FRIENDLY

I always say I prefer baking over cooking, because I'm not a technical person. I enjoy the creativity in the kitchen, but not the science behind it. When it comes to cooking, I can make a recipe and nail it on the first try, but with baking, it's more of a technical process. The chocolate cake on the back of the Hershey's cocoa jar is one of my favorite cakes, so I adapted the original version to make it more sophisticated in both flavor and presentation.

See photo on following page.

POACHED PEARS

3 cups	merlot
½ cup	honey
5	cloves
2	cinnamon sticks
3	strips orange zest
·	juice of 1 orange
4	firm, ripe Bosc pears, peeled, stems attached

1. **Prepare the poached pears:** Press cloves into orange zest strips. In a large saucepan, combine merlot, honey, cinnamon sticks, clove-studded orange zest, and orange juice. Bring the mixture to a boil, stirring to dissolve honey.

2. Add pears, reduce heat to a simmer; cook, uncovered, for 20-25 minutes, turning the pears after 10 minutes, until tender. Remove pears from the pan; set aside. Discard cinnamon sticks and clove-studded orange zest. Remove 1 cup wine; set aside.

3. Simmer remaining spiced wine until it has reduced to a syrup and coats the back of a spoon, 10-12 minutes.

RED WINE CHOCOLATE CAKE

2 cups	sugar
1¾ cups	flour
¾ cup	Dutch process cocoa powder
1½ tsp	baking powder
1½ tsp	baking soda
1 tsp	kosher salt
1 tsp	cinnamon
½ tsp	ground cloves
2	eggs
1 cup	almond milk
½ cup	canola oil
1½ tsp	vanilla extract
1 cup	reserved spiced wine

1. **Prepare the red wine chocolate cake:** Preheat oven to 350°F. Grease and flour a Bundt pan; set aside.

2. In a large bowl, combine sugar, flour, cocoa powder, baking powder, baking soda, salt, cinnamon, and cloves. Whisk to incorporate.

3. In a second bowl, combine eggs, almond milk, oil, and vanilla; whisk until creamy. Add the wet ingredients to the dry ingredients; mix well to incorporate. Add 1 cup spiced wine to the batter; stir to incorporate. Batter will be thin.

4. Bake for 45 minutes, or until a toothpick inserted into the center comes out clean. Cool for 15 minutes; unmold onto a cake stand. Cool completely before adding ganache.

GANACHE TOPPING

¼ cup   full-fat canned coconut milk

4 oz.   chocolate chips (¾ cup)

½ tsp   vanilla extract

1 Tbsp   wine syrup

pinch   sea salt

1. **Prepare the ganache topping:** In a small saucepan, bring coconut milk to a simmer. Place chocolate chips into a heatproof bowl; pour hot coconut milk over them. Let it stand for one minute.

2. Stir the chocolate until creamy; add vanilla, wine syrup, and sea salt.

3. Pour ganache over the cake.

FOR SERVING

- reserved poached pears
- toasted hazelnuts, chopped, for optional garnish
- wine syrup

1. For an elegant presentation, place poached pears into the center of the cake; garnish with chopped hazelnuts.

2. To serve, cut the pears into quarters and core them. Cut each quarter into thin slices, being careful not to cut all the way through so that the quarters are attached at the top (see photo, following page). Spread the slices to create a "fan"; serve with sliced chocolate cake and remaining wine syrup.

— FREEZING INSTRUCTIONS —

Wrap glazed cake airtight. Freezing pears and syrup is not recommended.

- QUICK AND EASY VARIATION -

Omit pears. Use leftover dry red wine (without aromatics) in the batter. Omit red wine syrup from the ganache.

——— TIP ———

Use a vegetable peeler to remove strips of zest from your orange.

——— NOTE ———

This cake is best prepared a few hours or 1 day in advance so the flavors have a chance to develop; the cake becomes more fudgy as it sits. Pour on the ganache and store, covered, at room temperature. Store pears and red wine syrup in the fridge until ready to serve.

SWEETS & TREATS

Babka Straws

Date Peanut Chews

Peanut Butter Banana Nice Cream

Cornbread Funnel Cakes

Marbled Halva Mousse

Pecan Pie Bites

Bourbon Roasted Peaches

Cowboy Biscotti

Chocolate Olive Oil Crinkle Gelt Cookies

Lemon Meltaways

Persimmon Fritters

Ice Cream Cone Bark

Pistachio Hot Chocolate

Babka STRAWS

PAREVE • YIELDS 4 DOZEN • FREEZER FRIENDLY

Babka is the millennial food trend that is not going away. I mean, what's not to love about yeasty cake with gooey chocolate? We've seen babkallah (babka challah) popularized in Bon Appetit magazine, babka bread pudding made famous by The New York Times, and babka French toast served up at Russ & Daughters. What you haven't seen till now are babka straws, and you can thank me later.

2 sheets	puff pastry, thawed
1 egg + 1 Tbsp	water, for egg wash

CHOCOLATE FILLING

1 cup	powdered sugar
½ cup	cocoa powder
1 tsp	vanilla extract
⅛ tsp	cinnamon
pinch	sea salt
¼ cup	canola oil
3 Tbsp	water

SWEET CRUMBS

1 cup	flour
1 cup	sugar
½ cup	canola oil
2 tsp	vanilla extract
pinch	sea salt

— NOTE —

If the dough becomes too soft to twist, place into refrigerator for about 10 minutes to firm up.

1. Line 3 baking sheets with parchment paper (work in batches, if necessary). Set aside. Preheat oven to 375°F.

2. **Prepare the chocolate filling:** In a small bowl, combine powdered sugar, cocoa powder, vanilla, cinnamon, sea salt, oil and water. Stir until creamy.

3. **Prepare the sweet crumbs:** In a second bowl, combine flour, sugar, oil, vanilla, and salt. Mix until crumbly.

4. **Prepare the babka straws:** Working with one sheet of puff pastry at a time, roll the dough out to form a large rectangle, about 12x17 inches. With the short side facing you, spread half of the chocolate mixture on the lower half of the dough; fold uncoated half over chocolate side.

5. Using a pizza cutter, cut the pastry into ½-inch strips. Twist the ends in opposite directions to give the straws a spiraled look. Transfer each strip to one of the baking sheets, spaced an inch or so apart. Refrigerate for 10 minutes. While straws are chilling, repeat with second sheet of puff pastry and the remaining chocolate filling.

6. Remove pans from the fridge; brush straws lightly with egg wash. Sprinkle with sweet crumbs.

7. Bake until puffed and golden, about 20 minutes.

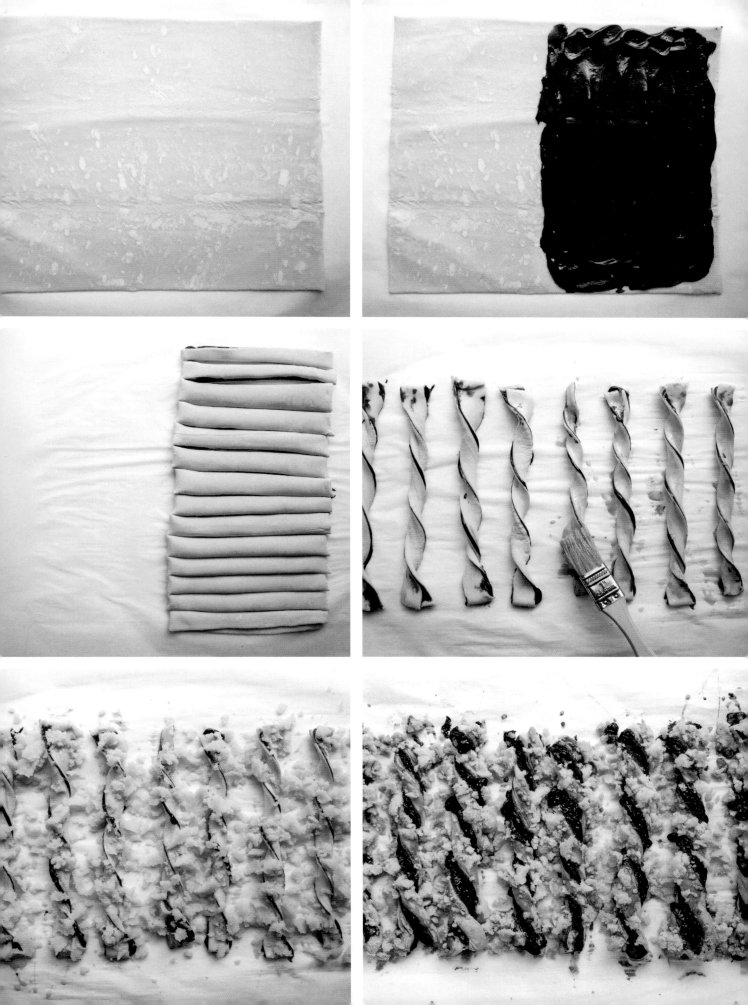

Date
PEANUT CHEWS

PAREVE · YIELDS APPROXIMATELY 20 PEANUT CHEWS · FREEZER FRIENDLY

We all have some type of nosh or candy that we associate with our childhood, and for me that's Nutty Chews. My bubby always had a bowl of them on her coffee table, and we'd stuff them into our pockets when she wasn't looking and sneak them home to eat later. I've always wanted to recreate them, and this guilt-free version is a home run. No sneaking necessary!

24	plump Medjool dates, pitted (about 1-lb.)
½ cup	salted roasted peanuts
8 oz.	chocolate chips
2 Tbsp	coconut oil or other neutral flavored oil
·	sea salt flakes, for topping

1. Line a baking sheet with parchment paper.

2. Add dates to a food processor; blend until a smooth paste forms. If needed, add a tiny splash of water.

3. With damp hands, remove the date paste from the food processor and place it on a piece of parchment paper. Knead the roasted peanuts into the date paste; re-wet hands if necessary. Roll mixture into a log that is ¾-inch high and 2-inches wide. Place log into the freezer for one hour or until solid.

4. Remove log from the freezer. Slice the log into ¾-inch slices (it helps to wipe your knife with a damp towel between slices so it doesn't stick). Freeze until solid.

5. In a double boiler, melt chocolate chips; stir in the oil. Remove date chews from the freezer; dip each piece into melted chocolate. Place on prepared baking sheet; sprinkle with sea salt flakes.

6. Refrigerate until solid; transfer chews to an airtight container. Keep frozen.

VARIATION

For quick and easy peanut chews, remove pits from dates and stuff with peanuts. Drizzle or dip in chocolate. Finish with sea salt flakes.

Peanut Butter Banana
NICE CREAM

PAREVE ▪ YIELDS 4-6 SERVINGS ▪ FREEZER FRIENDLY

Banana ice cream, or as Millennials have dubbed it, nice cream, has gotten me through many after-dinner sweet cravings. I've experimented with lots of different flavors, but this one takes the cake. The best part about banana ice cream is that you get to load on the toppings without the guilt. Add some chocolate chips and my peanut butter granola and it takes it over the top.

ICE CREAM

4	very ripe bananas
¼ cup	natural peanut butter
1 Tbsp	maple syrup, or to taste
pinch	cinnamon
pinch	sea salt

OPTIONAL TOPPINGS

- Peanut Butter Granola (page 52), cocoa nibs, melted chocolate, honey roasted peanuts

— VARIATION —

Use almond butter, tahini, chocolate hazelnut spread, or any nut butter instead of the peanut butter.

1. Peel and slice bananas. Place into a container or ziplock bag; freeze overnight.

2. Place frozen banana slices into a food processor fitted with the "S" blade or into a powerful blender; blend until smooth and creamy, scraping down the sides of the bowl as needed. Add peanut butter, maple syrup, cinnamon and sea salt; process until incorporated.

3. Serve immediately for soft-serve ice cream consistency or freeze until ready to serve. Thaw lightly to soften before serving.

Cornbread
FUNNEL CAKES

DAIRY OR PAREVE ▪ YIELDS APPROXIMATELY 7 FUNNEL CAKES

Funnel cakes are my dessert of choice for Chanukah. They are super fun to make (they don't call them FUNnel cakes for nothing!) and such a crowd pleaser! While traditional funnel cakes are definitely delicious, I dreamed up this cornbread version 'cuz cornbread-anything is my jam (and yes, you can even eat them with jam — see what I did there?).

1¼ cups	flour
¾ cup	cornmeal
⅓ cup	sugar
½ tsp	kosher salt
1 tsp	baking powder
2	eggs, lightly beaten
1 cup	whole milk OR nondairy milk
▪	canola oil, for frying
▪	powdered sugar, for dusting
▪	maple syrup, for dipping

1. In a mixing bowl, combine flour, cornmeal, sugar, salt, and baking powder. Add eggs and milk; and stir to combine. Place the batter into a piping or ziplock bag with one corner snipped off.

2. Heat a few inches of oil in a deep skillet. Squeeze a bit of batter into the oil to test for readiness. If batter rises to the top, the oil is hot enough.

3. Pipe about ⅓ cup batter in the hot oil in a circular motion to create a spiral pattern. Fry until golden; flip to fry the other side. Drain on paper towels. Repeat with remaining batter.

4. Dust funnel cakes with powdered sugar; serve immediately, with maple syrup for dipping.

Marbled Halva
MOUSSE

PAREVE ▪ YIELDS 10 (2-OZ.) SERVINGS ▪ FREEZER FRIENDLY

My zaidy always used to joke about his love for candy, and halva was his favorite. My mom would often send bags of chocolate-coated halva squares to him, but I never really got the appeal. That is, until I spent a year living in Israel. It's hard to walk past the Halva King stall in Machane Yehudah market without one of their crown-wearing workers ushering you into their sesame world. They've got halva in every flavor under the sun, from coffee to candied pecan and nougat. I definitely developed an appreciation for halva that year, and I took it back with me to the States, where I grew to love Zaidy's favorite candy.

8 oz.	whip topping, such as Rich Whip, thawed
½ cup	tahini
3 Tbsp	silan OR honey
1 tsp	vanilla extract
⅛ tsp	sea salt, or to taste
¼ cup	chocolate chips
▪	shredded halva, chopped pistachios, and sliced strawberries, for serving

1. In a mixer, beat the whip topping until stiff peaks form. Using a spatula, carefully fold in tahini, silan, and vanilla; season, to taste, with sea salt. Transfer half the mousse to a second bowl.

2. Melt chocolate chips in a double boiler or the microwave. Cool slightly. Fold chocolate into half of the mousse.

3. For a marbled effect, fill a piping bag so that the vanilla mousse is to the left of the bag and the chocolate mousse is to the right. Pipe into mousse cups. Alternatively, place the flavors into two separate bags and pipe in layers of chocolate and vanilla. Top with shredded halva, chopped pistachos, and sliced strawberries.

VARIATION

Layer in a container; freeze. Serve frozen for halva ice cream.

Pecan Pie
BITES

PAREVE ▪ YIELDS 18-20 BITES ▪ FREEZER FRIENDLY

Date truffles are a Shabbos staple in my home, especially during the summer months when we always need healthy snacks on hand for the long days. I love to play around with different combinations of dates, nuts, and spices; my marzipan flavor has become a much-loved staple for many of my followers. This pecan pie version is hard to resist, and it keeps really well in the fridge for those late-night cravings.

10	plump Medjool dates (8 oz.)
5 oz.	pecans (1 heaping cup)
1 tsp	vanilla extract
¼ tsp	cinnamon
▪	sea salt, to taste
▪	honey roasted pecans, for topping
⅓ cup	chocolate chips, optional, for drizzling
▪	sea salt flakes, for finishing

1. Using a food processor fitted with the "S" blade, process dates, pecans, vanilla, cinnamon, and sea salt until a dough forms. Don't overprocess the mixture or the nuts will begin to release their natural oils and the mixture will become oily.

2. Roll the dough into small balls; press a pecan into each ball.

3. If desired, melt the chocolate chips by putting them into a ziplock bag and placing the bag into a bowl of boiling water until the chocolate has melted. Snip the corner of the bag; drizzle the chocolate over the pecan bites. Finish with sea salt flakes, if desired.

4. Store in the refrigerator for up to 2 weeks.

— TIP —

If your dates are not very moist, soak them in a bowl of hot water for about 10 minutes to rehydrate them before using.

Bourbon Roasted
PEACHES

PAREVE ▪ YIELDS 4 SERVINGS ▪ FREEZER FRIENDLY

Roasting is the cooking method of choice for vegetables, but often overlooked for fruit; you usually find fruits cooked down into compotes or jams, but roasting them is seriously underrated. I love how the sweet flavor of the fruit caramelizes and intensifies in the oven, and these bourbon-roasted peaches are among my best summertime desserts.

4 large	peaches, sliced
¼ cup	brown sugar
2 Tbsp	bourbon

- sea salt, to taste
- Coconut Whipped Cream, for serving (see below)
- chopped nuts OR crushed spiced cookies (such as gingersnaps or Lotus), optional, for serving

1. Preheat oven to 400°F.

2. Spread peaches on a baking sheet; toss with brown sugar, bourbon, and salt.

3. Bake for 30 minutes, stirring occasionally, until the peaches are tender and the syrup is thick and syrupy.

4. Serve warm with Coconut Whipped Cream and nuts or cookies, if desired.

COCONUT WHIPPED CREAM

1 (14-oz.) can	full-fat coconut milk, refrigerated for 24 hours
1-2 Tbsp	powdered sugar, maple syrup, OR honey, to taste (see Note)
½ tsp	vanilla extract

1. Carefully, without shaking it, remove the can of coconut milk from the refrigerator. Open the can; use a spoon to remove the thick layer of coconut cream from the top of the can. Transfer it to your mixing bowl. (Do not use the layer of coconut water that has settled to the bottom of the can.)

2. In a mixer, beat the coconut cream on medium speed for 2-3 minutes, or until the cream becomes light and fluffy and peaks form. Add powdered sugar and vanilla extract; beat until incorporated.

3. Serve immediately, or transfer to a sealed container and refrigerate until ready to use.

--- NOTE ---

Powdered sugar will help the whipped cream hold its shape, while honey or maple syrup will thin it out slightly.

Cowboy BISCOTTI

PAREVE • YIELDS 3 DOZEN BISCOTTI • FREEZER FRIENDLY

Cowboy cookies are a real Busy in Brooklyn #oldiebutgoodie. The recipe, which I first read about in Martha Stewart's magazine, is chock full of coconut, pecans, chocolate, and oats. I have to admit, I don't really know why they go by that name, but it's a cute one, so I let it stick. Fast forward a few years and I brought the cookies back, in the healthy form of a cookie dough bite; this time I've re-imagined it in the form of biscotti.

2 cups	flour
1½ cups	old-fashioned oats
1 tsp	baking powder
1 cup	sugar
½ tsp	kosher salt
1 cup	oil
2	eggs
1 tsp	vanilla extract
⅔ cup	mini chocolate chips
⅓ cup	unsweetened shredded coconut
½ cup	chopped pecans

— NOTE —

If you wish to make larger biscotti, form the dough into one large log instead of two.

1. Preheat oven to 350°F. Line 2 baking sheets with parchment paper.

2. In a large mixing bowl, combine flour, oats, baking powder, sugar, and salt; whisk until incorporated.

3. In a second bowl, combine oil, eggs, and vanilla; whisk until smooth. Add wet ingredients to dry ingredients; mix until a batter forms. Stir in chocolate chips, coconut, and pecans.

4. Divide dough in half. Transfer each piece of dough to a prepared baking sheet; form each into a log. Bake for 30 minutes, or until lightly golden.

5. Remove from oven; cool for 15 minutes. Lower the oven temperature to 300°F.

6. Slice log crosswise into ½-inch slices. Place slices on the baking sheet; bake for 25 minutes, or until lightly toasted.

Chocolate Olive Oil
CRINKLE GELT COOKIES

PAREVE • YIELDS 3-4 DOZEN COOKIES • FREEZER FRIENDLY

I've always been very creative but until I started blogging, I never quite found the right channel for that creativity. I enjoy blogging so much because it challenges me to think outside the box. The holidays are my favorite time to get creative and these Crinkle Gelt Cookies are among my most prized recipes. We all associate Chanukah with chocolate gelt, and I'll never forget how one year, after Chanukah, my son brought me a quarter and asked me unwrap it! Unwrapping the gold foil wrapper is what inspired my gold-foiled crinkle cookies, and adding the fruity olive oil and Dutch process cocoa powder really make these extra rich, fudgy, and appropriate for the holiday.

2 cups	flour
1 cup	Dutch process cocoa powder
2 tsp	baking powder
½ tsp	kosher salt
⅔ cup	extra virgin olive oil
2 cups	sugar
2	eggs
2 tsp	vanilla extract
2 tsp	coffee dissolved in ¼ cup hot water
•	Wilton gold color mist food spray
•	bittersweet chocolate gelt coins, unwrapped

NOTES

If you prefer not to use olive oil, you may use canola or any neutral-flavored oil instead.

If cookies are frozen with chocolate coins, the coins may discolor slightly but that will not affect taste.

VARIATION

Spray the cookies with silver color mist; top with milk chocolate coins. If you prefer not to use color mist, roll the cookies in turbinado or powdered sugar instead.

1. Preheat oven to 350°F. Line 2 baking sheets with parchment paper.

2. In a bowl, whisk together flour, cocoa, baking powder, and salt.

3. In a second bowl, combine olive oil, sugar, eggs, vanilla, and coffee mixture.

4. Add the dry ingredients to the wet ingredients; stir well to combine. If any lumps remain, stir the mixture with a hand-mixer until all the ingredients are well incorporated. Place the dough in the refrigerator for a few hours or overnight.

5. Roll 1 tablespoon of chilled dough into a ball; place on a prepared baking sheet. Roll the dough quickly so that the heat of your hands does not make it sticky. Repeat with remaining dough.

6. Spray the cookies with gold mist food spray (do not spray near the open oven door, as color sprays are flammable); bake for approximately 15 minutes. Set aside to cool.

7. While the cookies are still a little warm (but not so hot that they melt the chocolate), press chocolate coins into the center of each cookie.

Lemon MELTAWAYS

PAREVE ▪ YIELDS 2 DOZEN COOKIES ▪ FREEZER FRIENDLY

When I was growing up, my mom used to make those crescent-shaped almond cookies that were dusted in powdered sugar and melted on your tongue. They always disappeared right out of the oven. While the cookies are a favorite of mine, the margarine we used to make them is not, so I stopped eating them … until the coconut oil craze happened. Coconut oil is one of the best things to happen to the kosher market because it allows you to replace butter in both solid and liquid form. Many people are put off by the coconut flavor, but if you buy refined coconut oil (Spectrum is my preferred brand), it does not have a coconut flavor at all. Somehow, the coconut oil (and the lemon!) takes these meltaways to a whole new level, and they melt on your tongue even more than the crescent-shaped cookies of my youth.

2 cups	flour
¼ cup	cornstarch
¾ cup	powdered sugar
½ tsp	kosher salt
1 cup	refined coconut oil, softened
1 Tbsp	lemon juice
1 Tbsp	lemon zest, lightly packed (from two lemons)
1 tsp	vanilla
2-3 Tbsp	powdered sugar, for dusting

1. Preheat oven to 350°F. Line a baking sheet with parchment paper.

2. In a large mixing bowl, combine flour, cornstarch, powdered sugar, and salt.

3. Add coconut oil, lemon juice, lemon zest, and vanilla. Stir until ingredients start to come together, then knead with your hands until a dough forms.

4. Place heaping tablespoons of dough on prepared baking sheets. Bake for 15 minutes, until lightly browned on the bottom.

5. Cool completely before handling. Dust cookies with powdered sugar to coat.

Persimmon FRITTERS

DAIRY ▪ YIELDS 10 SERVINGS

Persimmon is one of the lesser-known fruits and I'm determined to share it with the world. What most people don't realize is that there are a few varieties and there are different ways to eat each one. Fuyu and hachiya are the most widely available types of persimmon. The fuyu, which I use in this recipe, look like tomatoes, and they are eaten unripe for an irresistible crunch. The hachiya, on the other hand, must be extremely ripe before eating, and I like to freeze them for a few hours (once they are super ripe and mushy) for instant creamy sorbet. Because persimmon become available around the same time as apple season, I decided to fry them up in the same fashion as apple fritters, for a super fun twist on one of my favorite fruits.

5	large fuyu persimmon, cut into ¼-inch-thick rings (peeling optional)
1½ cups	flour
¼ cup	sugar
½ tsp	cinnamon
1 tsp	baking powder
pinch	salt
1¼ cups	milk
1	egg
▪	canola oil, for frying

COATING

½ cup	sugar
1 tsp	cinnamon

1. In a bowl, whisk together flour, sugar, cinnamon, baking powder, and salt. In a separate bowl, mix together milk and egg. Add the wet ingredients to the dry; stir until a thick batter forms.

2. In a shallow bowl, mix together sugar and cinnamon.

3. Heat a few inches of oil in a heavy saucepan over medium heat. Drop a spoonful of batter into the oil to test for readiness. If batter rises to the top, the oil is hot enough.

4. Coat persimmon rings with batter, shaking excess back into bowl. Drop rings, a few at a time, into hot oil; fry on each side until golden and puffy. Remove with tongs or a slotted spoon; drain on paper towels. Toss in cinnamon-sugar mixture. Serve hot.

NOTE

You may also use this batter to make fried Oreos or funnel cakes.

VARIATION

For a fun Chanukah treat, cut out the centers of the persimmon rings with an apple corer so that they resemble donuts; fry as above.

Ice Cream Cone BARK

DAIRY ▪ YIELDS 10 SERVINGS ▪ FREEZER FRIENDLY

I did the bulk of my recipe testing for this book last summer, in the modest kitchen of my summer home in upstate New York. The best part of testing recipes in a bungalow colony is that I shared all the food with my neighbors so I could get feedback. Not surprisingly, this ice cream cone bark was a huge hit with everyone, and my kids have been begging me to make it again ever since!

12 oz.	dairy white chocolate
3 Tbsp	colored sprinkles
3	sugar cones, crushed

1. Melt chocolate over a double boiler; using an offset spatula, spread it into an even layer on a parchment-lined baking sheet. Sprinkle chocolate with colored sprinkles and crushed sugar cones; chill until set.

2. Break chocolate into pieces. Store in an airtight container for up to two weeks.

Pistachio
HOT CHOCOLATE

DAIRY ▪ YIELDS 4 SERVINGS

Nut milks are all the rage right now, with flavors ranging from cashew to macadamia and hazelnut milk. They are a great alternative to the soy milk we grew up on and are pretty easy to make yourself! All you need is a high-powered blender and a nut milk bag, and you'll be on your way to creamy and dreamy pareve milk.

1 cup	raw unsalted pistachios
2 cups	water
1 Tbsp	honey
1 tsp	vanilla
pinch	sea salt
1 oz.	white chocolate
▪	edible rose petals, optional garnish

ORANGE CARDAMOM WHIPPED CREAM

½ cup	heavy cream
1 Tbsp	powdered sugar
1 tsp	orange zest
pinch	ground cardamom, or to taste

1. **Prepare the cardamom whipped cream:** Using an electric mixer, beat together heavy cream, sugar, orange zest, and cardamom until stiff peaks form. Place into refrigerator until ready to use.

2. **Prepare the hot chocolate:** In a high-powered blender, blend the pistachios and water until creamy. Place a nut milk bag over a small saucepan; pour pistachio milk into it. Squeeze the nut milk bag to remove as much of the milk as possible. Discard the pistachio pulp in the bag (see Note).

3. Add honey, vanilla, and sea salt to the milk; bring to a simmer. Add chocolate; stir until melted.

4. Divide the milk between four cups. Top with orange cardamom whipped cream; garnish with rose petals, if desired.

— NOTES —

The thickness of the pistachio milk will vary, depending on the strength of your blender and how much you are able to extract from the bag. If the milk is too thick for your liking, you can adjust the consistency by adding more water.

Nut milk bags are mesh straining bags that enable you to easily extract milk from nuts and seeds. They are available online.

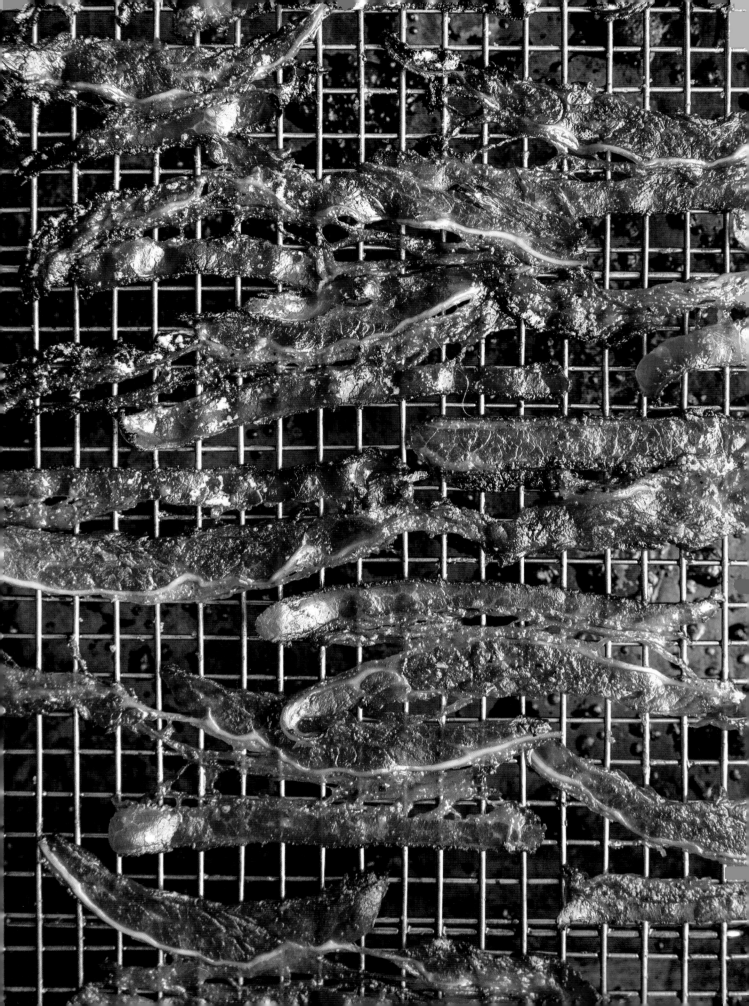

Sweet & Smoky
POPCORN

MEAT ▪ YIELDS 8-10 CUPS

Who doesn't love freshly popped corn — it smells delicious, it's light (if you don't eat the whole bag), it's inexpensive, and it's easy to make! Of course you can throw a bag into your microwave and get poppin' but just a little bit of effort is gonna give you a whole lot of reward with this recipe. It's worth it.

¼ cup	brown sugar
1 (6-oz.) pkg.	beef fry
½ cup	popcorn kernels

SPICE MIX

5 Tbsp	neutral-flavored oil
2 Tbsp	smoked paprika
2 Tbsp	brown sugar
2 tsp	chili powder
½ tsp	kosher salt

VARIATION

To make the popcorn pareve, omit the beef fry and use 1 tablespoon neutral-flavored oil instead of the drippings.

1. **Prepare the beef fry:** Place ¼ cup brown sugar into a ziplock bag. Add beef fry slices, one at a time, shaking the bag to evenly coat with sugar. Place beef fry on a rack set over a baking sheet; bake at 400° for 10-15 minutes, until crispy. Cool completely; chop into bite-size pieces. Reserve drippings on baking sheet.

2. **Prepare the spice mix:** Combine oil, smoked paprika, brown sugar, chili powder, and kosher salt in a bowl. Set aside.

3. **Prepare the popcorn:** Pour the drippings from the sheet tray into a heavy-bottomed pot (you should have about 1 tablespoon; if you don't have enough, add more oil to equal 1 tablespoon). Heat the pot over medium heat; add one popcorn kernel to the pot to test oil for readiness. When the kernel pops, the oil is hot enough. Pour the rest of the kernels into the pot; cover.

4. Shake the pot over the heat, keeping it covered, until the corn stops popping. Remove the pot from the heat.

5. Transfer popcorn to a large bowl. Pour the spice mix over popcorn; stir to coat. Stir in the chopped beef fry.

Roasted Chickpeas, THREE WAYS

DAIRY OR PAREVE · YIELDS 1½ CUPS EACH

I've been making roasted chickpeas since before roasted chickpeas became a thing. My kids grew up on them, and they helped me make it through Stage 1 of the South Beach Diet more times than I can count. Honestly, you don't even need a recipe for these; they're great with any spice, but here are the ones that we like best.

1 (15-oz.) can	chickpeas, drained, rinsed, and patted dry
1 Tbsp	olive oil
·	flavoring of choice (see below)

TACO SPICE MIX
PAREVE

1 tsp	chili powder
½ tsp	cumin
½ tsp	smoked paprika
¼ tsp	onion powder
¼ tsp	garlic powder
pinch	cayenne pepper
·	salt, to taste

FALAFEL SPICE MIX
PAREVE

1½ tsp	cumin
1 tsp	coriander
½ tsp	onion powder
½ tsp	garlic powder
·	salt, to taste

PIZZA SPICE MIX
DAIRY OR PAREVE

1 Tbsp	Parmesan cheese OR nutritional yeast, plus more for dusting
1 tsp	oregano
½ tsp	garlic powder
2 Tbsp	tomato paste
⅛ tsp	pepper
·	salt, to taste

1. Preheat oven to 400°F. Spread chickpeas on a baking sheet; toss with oil and desired spice mix.

2. Bake for about 40-45 minutes, shaking the pan once or twice during baking, until crispy.

3. Before serving, cool for a few minutes to crisp.

——— NOTE ———

For best results, do not line baking sheet with parchment paper.

Slice & Bake
BISCUIT COOKIES

PAREVE ▪ YIELDS 2 DOZEN COOKIES ▪ FREEZER FRIENDLY

Of all the recipes in the book, this one is probably the most "out of the box" — in concept at least. I was inspired to make a cookie reminiscent of kishke — not the REAL intestine stuff — the cracker or cornflake variations we've come to love in our cholent. The result was not quite a kishke cookie, but more of a black pepper biscuit. Taste testers weren't sure what they were eating — but the reviews were unanimous — you just can't stop eating them!

1½ cups	flour
½ cup	cornflake crumbs
1 tsp	baking powder
1 tsp	kosher salt
1 tsp	coarsely ground black pepper
½ cup	sugar
⅓ cup	oil
2	eggs

1. Preheat oven to 350°F. Line a baking sheet with parchment paper.

2. In a mixing bowl, combine flour, cornflake crumbs, baking powder, salt, black pepper, and sugar.

3. In a second bowl, combine oil and eggs. Add the wet ingredients to the dry ingredients; stir until ingredients start to come together, then knead with your hands until a dough forms.

4. Form the dough into 2 logs, approximately 1½-inch in diameter; wrap each in parchment paper, twisting on each end to tighten. Refrigerate for 1 hour. Unwrap log; cut log into ½-inch thick slices. Repeat with second log.

5. Place slices on prepared baking sheet; bake for 15-18 minutes, until the underside is browned. Cool completely to crisp up before serving.

Honey Za'atar
GRANOLA CLUSTERS

PAREVE ▪ YIELDS 5-6 CUPS ▪ FREEZER FRIENDLY

Granola is a great snack because of its crunch factor, but I'm hard-pressed to find a brand that is not too sweet. I don't like chocolate chips or cranberries in my mix — just pure toasted oat bliss, and these clusters deliver. If you like my honey zaatar roasted chicken (page 166), you're gonna love these!

½ cup	honey
½ cup	olive oil
4 cups	old-fashioned oats
1½ cups	sliced almonds
½ cup	sesame seeds
3 Tbsp	za'atar
1 tsp	kosher salt

1. Preheat oven to 300°F. Line a baking sheet with parchment paper.

2. In a small saucepan, melt together honey and olive oil. In a large bowl, combine the oats, almonds, sesame seeds, za'atar, and salt. Add honey mixture; stir to coat evenly.

3. Spread mixture onto prepared baking sheet. Bake for 20 minutes, stir, and bake an additional 25 minutes. Cool completely for one hour; break into clusters.

─── VARIATION ───

You may replace some of the oats with equal parts pistachios or sunflower seeds.

─── SERVING SUGGESTION ───

Enjoy with labneh and dried fruits such as apricots, figs, or dates.

Herbes de Provence
TWICE-ROASTED CHESTNUTS

PAREVE ▪ YIELDS 10 OUNCES

I used to wait all year for chestnut season to come around so I could roast them. They are not the easiest to work with, so when they started selling bags of roasted chestnuts on the kosher market, I was elated. Do you know what's better than prepared roasted chestnuts? Roasting them twice. Herbes de Provence — a seasoning blend with several variations often including dried savory, fennel, lavender, thyme, and basil — gives the chestnuts some crunch and a savory boost in flavor.

2 (5.2-oz.) bags   roasted chestnuts
1 Tbsp   olive oil
1 tsp   herbes de Provence
½ tsp   kosher salt

1. Preheat oven to 375°F. On a baking sheet, stir the chestnuts with oil, herbs, and salt to coat.

2. Bake for 15-20 minutes until crispy. Serve immediately.

Smoky Sumac
ALMONDS

PAREVE ▪ YIELDS APPROXIMATELY 1½ CUPS ▪ FREEZER FRIENDLY

Sumac is one of those Middle Eastern spices that just doesn't get the attention it deserves, at least not here in the U.S., and not yet anyway. The spice is tangy, pungent, not to mention beautifully crimson, and I'm hoping you're all inspired to add it to your spice shelf. A pinch on top of runny eggs, a teaspoon in salad dressing, or a sprinkle in your tahini goes a long way.

10 oz.	almonds (scant 2 cups)
1 Tbsp	olive oil
2 Tbsp	liquid smoke
1 Tbsp	sumac
1 tsp	kosher salt
½ tsp	chili pepper flakes

1. Preheat oven to 300°F. Line a baking sheet with parchment paper.

2. In a small bowl, toss almonds with olive oil, liquid smoke, sumac, salt, and chili pepper flakes. Spread the nuts on prepared baking sheet; bake for 30 minutes, stirring once during baking.

3. Cool completely to crisp up before serving.

— NOTE —

Liquid smoke is available in major supermarkets.

Furikake
EDAMAME

PAREVE ▪ YIELDS 4 SERVINGS

Furikake is a savory Japanese seasoning that usually includes nori, bonito flakes, sesame, and red chili flakes. I use dried mushroom powder in place of the nonkosher bonito for a kosher umami boost. Use the mix on edamame, sushi rice, or popcorn!

14 oz.	frozen edamame in the pod
▪	salt
▪	soy sauce, to taste

FURIKAKE SEASONING

1 sheet	nori
1 tsp	porcini mushroom powder
½ tsp	red pepper flakes
½ tsp	kosher salt
pinch	sugar, optional
1 Tbsp	mixed toasted sesame seeds

--- NOTE ---

Store any extra furikake seasoning in an airtight container for up to 3 months.

--- VARIATION ---

You may process half the furikake mixture in a spice grinder for a more finely ground blend.

1. **Prepare the edamame:** Fill a large saucepan with salted water; bring to a boil. Add edamame and cook for 5 minutes, until bright green and tender. Remove edamame with a slotted spoon; place into a bowl of ice water to stop the cooking.

2. With tongs, hold nori sheet over an open flame or electric burner, moving it slowly over the heat to toast it. Cut the nori into very small strips.

3. **Prepare the furikake seasoning:** Combine nori, mushroom powder, red pepper flakes, salt, optional sugar, and sesame seeds.

4. Drain edamame; season, to taste, with soy sauce. Sprinkle with furikake seasoning to taste.

INDEX

SPECIAL THANKS

Benz's Gourmet
Hostess International
Godinger Silver Art Co.
On the Table, Teaneck
Myrtle & Rum

Timeless Table
Lulus Gallery of Gifts
Sharon Sabbagh
Shlomie Klein, Mr. Greens
Naf & Anna Hanau, Grow and Behold

Maggy Rogatsky @couturespaces
Chaya Goldstein @homeit_organizing
Rachel Adler Designs